11/01

THE
ULTIMATE
CHEESE-CAKE
COOKBOOK

THE ULTIMATE CHEESE-CAKE COOKBOOK

Joey Reynolds

with Myra Chanin

ST. MARTIN'S GRIFFIN
NEW YORK

www.stmartins.com

Design by Kathryn Parise

LIBRARY OF CONGRESS CATALOGING-IN-PUBLICATION DATA
Reynolds, Joey.
    The ultimate cheesecake cookbook / Joey Reynolds,
    with Myra Chanin.—1st ed.
        p. cm.
    ISBN 0-312-27128-X
    1. Cheesecake (Cookery) I. Chanin, Myra. II. Title.

TX773 .R49 2001
641.8′653—dc21   00-045870

First Edition: May 2001

10 9 8 7 6 5 4 3 2 1

This book is dedicated to the one I love, Homer Simpson, the only person to successfully get Mother Wonderful to stop talking. Can you imagine how insulting it is to be told what to do by a cartoon? Rarely is it that a coauthor dedicates a book to his coauthor, but we are sewn at the lip on my radio show. The truth of the matter is that Myra Chanin (Mother Wonderful) has an opinion on everything, even this dedication. God forbid that she gets to edit it! I have said that if she were bound and gagged, she would find a way to speak intravenously. You gotta love her. There is no better sport, charming hostess, compassionate person, and greater friend than Myra. Who else has 150 cheesecake recipes and is willing to share them?

—JOEY REYNOLDS

This book is dedicated to my great friend Joey Reynolds, who lets me run my mouth every Friday night on his radio show. It's also dedicated to his devoted listeners, who call to defend me whenever he verbally abuses me. I want to assure you all, he doesn't really mean it. He's a wonderfully funny, smart, and insightful human being. Who else do you know who has four million listeners and is willing to share them?

—MYRA CHANIN

Contents

"Love is the willingness to look like you're the one who wanted dessert."

"Life is learning to accept Plan B."

"Remember that overnight success usually takes 15 years."

"I come from a dysfunctional family. I was born after Adam and Eve."

Introduction

$\int$orget chicken soup—cheesecake is good for your soul. Every time you make, serve, and eat a cheesecake, great things will happen. You will perform random acts of kindness. You will love your neighbors in spite of bratty kids, barking dogs, and other annoying qualities. You will not scream obscenities at people who cut you off on the freeway. You will find no fault in your husbands, wives, girlfriends, boyfriends, or significant others. You will understand the meaning of life. You will do your part to make the world a better place.

One of the keys to making a good cheesecake is using the finest ingredients. Don't think you are clever by buying your cream cheese in bulk at your local generic food club. Brands matter and quality is a must. Use only fresh ingredients if you don't want your cake tasting like the leftovers decaying in your refrigerator. Foods *do* pick up strong flavors if they are left to languish too long without being used. It is a very sad thing. Buy what you need right before you intend to use it—unless, of course, you have a middle-of-the-night cheesecake emergency. In that case, you probably don't care if the cake is perfect or not. You are probably planning to eat it yourself. It happens—be prepared.

But do not let the recipes in these pages limit your cheesecake creativity. Once you learn the basics, there can be a cheesecake for every occasion. And don't be afraid of flops. My Y2cake could have been a disaster.

Mangia!

—Joey Reynolds

The Joey of Cheesecake

Myra Chanin, also known as Mother Wonderful, is responsible for all of the grunt work in this book. The Joey Reynolds Cheesecake would not have been made possible if it were not for Myra and her sweetness and her dedication. She was my dealer, because I consider cheesecake a drug.

I'll never forget how I first met her. She was Rollerblading to WFIL in Philadelphia and carrying a couple of cakes. I think she got a DUI for it.

Myra created her piña colada cake when I was a young man in Philadelphia, and that was a long time ago. She forced me to eat her piña colada cake. One bite of her cake, and I went into multiple orgasms. I was swinging from the Liberty Bell yelling "Give me some more!" And that's how I met Myra. She was great.

Myra created designer cheesecakes. She had all the principles down and I learned them from her. Myra made a lot of different designer cakes in different flavors, and years later I came up with mine based on her principles. But it was by accident that my cake was created. It had nothing to do with Mother Wonderful. It had to do with single parenting.

While living as a single parent to my two lovely daughters, it was up to me to do the things I had always relied on my ex-wife to do. For example, when my church had its potluck social, it was up to me to bring a covered dish or whatever people bring to church potlucks. Well, I figured the world could do without one more Waldorf salad or Jell-O mold.

I wanted to make an impression. After all, I was the only man bringing food, and besides that, I am Italian. It is a measure of an Italian man how well he can cook. I decided on Key lime pie but realized, when it was far too late to do anything about it, that I was lacking some very "key" ingredients. My two young angels were sleeping, so I resorted to a little bit of this and a lot more of that. And there was evening, and there was morning, and thus on the seventh day the Joey Key Lime Cheesecake was born.

It was a big hit and everyone wanted more. There was only one problem: I couldn't remember what was in it. I tried recreating the circumstances, asking my daughters to pretend they were asleep. After trial and error, I was able to recreate the recipe in this book. Of course, I was hooked, and you will find several other original Joey recipes.

Although I think we have covered almost every cheesecake from here to eternity, feel free to be creative. Cheesecake should never take the place of professional therapy or medical advice. However, it has been determined through anecdotal studies to have a highly beneficial effect on one's mental and physical state.

Enjoy!

About Myra Chanin

I'm a cookbook author whose specialty is cheesecake, the baked kind. I became a professional baker because my husband Alvin and I were not getting along after six years of marriage.

Even more unnerving than the threat of divorce was the prospect of job hunting. The openings available to an English major with a spotty employment record hardly coincided with my fantasies. I was offered only positions as a substitute teacher when, in my heart, I knew I deserved to be ruler of the world. Since I didn't take direction well, I knew I'd have to become self-employed. The only road to independence led through my kitchen. I was an excellent cook and a decent baker.

Philadelphia was in the throes of a restaurant renaissance. Many fine young chefs had managed to open small dining rooms on a shoestring. They could barely pay the rent, let alone hire a full-time baker. I supplied desserts to these brand-new restaurateurs.

It began with my lunching at Philadelphia's Fish Market, which eventually became a large nationally lauded gourmet restaurant, but then it seated twenty at five tables in the rear. I told the owner I made a better cheesecake than the one he served. He said, "Show me." If he agreed, he'd buy them from me. I presented him with my first creation, flavored with chutzpah. How did he like it? He didn't. The brute actually claimed it gave him heartburn! I've always believed that No! didn't mean never. So, I returned to my mixer to try and try again. The owner loved the lime-almond cheesecake I brought him the following week. So did his customers. Voilà! An entrepreneur was born.

Soon more restaurateurs began knocking on my door, and I branched out into more complex cakes and cookies. I dazzled clients with exotic flavors: Ginger Pear, Mocha Blanca, Honey Fig. Naming the cakes properly was three-fourths of the battle. My products won Philly's Best awards, and for the first time I was recognized as somebody wonderful—Mother Wonderful—a woman who not only could support herself, but who could make the world a sweeter place.

My business thrived, but as my baking repertoire expanded, so did my waistline. In Mother Wonderful's kitchen, batter was wiped from fingers by human lips—mine! New recipes took on lives of their own.

So did my marriage collapse? No. It's actually thriving! Alvin and I are still in love after more than thirty-four years.

Did cheesecake keep my marriage together? It didn't hurt it. It's impossible for anyone who enjoys fine food as much as my husband does to stay mad at the hand that feeds him. Alvin may want to get away from me from time to time, but he'll never desert my cheesecakes.

If you want to get or stay married, cheesecake is a tried-and-tested route. I know that relationships are supposed to be equal, but the classic approach to connubial bliss has always been 50 percent culinary. The reason everyone says the way to a man's heart is through his stomach is because we all know that it isn't through his brains. Soft lights, sweet music, and lingerie from Victoria's Secret may create an evening's diversion, but comes the dawn, all men must eat. The woman or creative man who serves a sensuous cheesecake will always have a devoted lover. So feed the man or woman in your life rich desserts and sauces made with heavy cream, and he or she will cleave to you forever.

Sex has limitations. Cheesecake is forever.

The Kosher Stuff

The Decadent Joey Reynolds Cheesecake is kosher. It is made in Florida at a kosher bakery and has papers—but it is dairy, not pareve. The Tofu Cheesecake is automatically kosher AND pareve. The restaurants in New York City that observe dietary laws want the tofu cake. They can't handle the Joey Reynolds Decadent Cheesecake if they sell meat products, and they can't put the dairy product next to it, but the tofu cake seems to be for all seasons.

THE
ULTIMATE
CHEESE-
CAKE
COOKBOOK

THE CHEESECAKE GOSPEL

READ BEFORE BAKING!

*C*heesecake is the easiest dessert to make!

How did it get such an awesome reputation? Bakers lie. When you find out how easy it is to make cheesecake, you'll stop paying $25 for theirs and start baking your own.

Bakers pass on anxiety-producing instructions that tell you to let your cheesecake sit in the oven after it's baked for 78 minutes with the door ajar. Utter nonsense! If the cake is done, it can go right into the fridge. If it isn't, it should be baked longer.

Even worse are those recipes that tell you to put your cheesecake pan in a pan filled with boiling water—a baking principle we think was devised by the marketing director of some pharmaceutical company who hoped to double the sales of adhesive bandages and first-aid sprays. We've never removed one of those from the oven without acquiring several blisters when hot water sloshed out of the pot and onto our delicate arms.

Cheesecakes should be custardlike in the middle and creamy around the edges. Why do people overbake them? Mostly because they're afraid they'll fall apart when they're shifted from the metal bottom of the springform pan onto a serving plate. On the other hand, if you're taking a cheesecake to a party or picnic, transporting and serving it on the original metal springform bottom usually rewards you with yet another tambourine ring when the bottom disappears. Solution: Before you start to bake, put the metal bottom plate that comes with the springform pan away in your closet. Buy a cardboard round from a baking-supply or paper goods store that's the same size as the metal bottom, and wrap the cardboard round in a sheet of heavy-duty aluminum foil. Use the foil-wrapped cardboard round to replace the metal bottom, and bake on this instead. You can even cut out a round from a corrugated box that's lying around your house. And if the foil-wrapped round isn't a perfect fit, trim the excess cardboard with a scissors or knife.

You can protect your oven from butter leaks simply by wrapping a second sheet of heavy-duty foil around the outside bottom rim of the springform pan and baking away. It's a good idea to do this even if you bake in a springform with the original metal bottom. Butter tends to leak out of these pans unless they are brand-new.

When the cheesecake is ready to serve, remove the cake ON ITS FOIL-LINED ROUND, put a paper doily under it, and place it on a tray or carry it to your destination. Baking cheesecakes on foil-wrapped rounds helps to cement friendships because your original metal bottoms don't get lost in the back of someone's cupboard, and if they do, you know how to replace them and keep your pans viable.

The subtleties of flavorings always make these cheesecakes exceptional. Many of these baked cheesecakes have been featured in restaurants and have won prizes through the years. Now we're passing all our secrets on to you in this book. Every one of these cheesecakes can be stored—uncut and boxed—in the refrigerator for seven days, and they can all be frozen for several months. We suggest that you freeze leftovers after you've served the cake at a dinner party. Left too long in the refrigerator, the sour-cream glaze on baked cheesecakes deteriorates first. It develops an unappetizing yellow tinge and dries out around the edges, so that you don't want to eat it, although you really could. If you freeze the leftovers, the glaze stays creamy. It's very little trouble to cut when it's frozen. Just use a sharp knife that you've run some hot water over and wiped dry.

Finally, we want to answer the question that people always ask us: Which cheesecake is our favorite? Our reply has always been the same: whichever one we happen to be feasting on.

CHAPTER 2

CHOICES

*O*ur grandmothers taught us that the three most important elements of cooking were ingredients, ingredients, and ingredients. Even when times were hard, in the middle of the Great Depression, they always turned up their noses at the weekly special and asked their food purveyors for the best quality of anything that they stocked.

After the merchants displayed the cream of their wares, our grandmothers always asked them a second question: "How much?" and then always gave the same comment to any reply they received: "Are you crazy? You want me to take out a mortgage to buy a pound of ground meat?" But everyone knew they were going to buy the best.

We do believe that quality costs more and we advise you to follow our lead. We want to give you the benefit of our experience by recommending some of our favorite ingredients here.

For crumb crusts, we prefer Nabisco 'Nilla Wafers because they grind up very finely. We think Nabisco Famous Chocolate Wafers are the absolute tops. Unfortunately, Nabisco Famous Chocolate Wafers are off limits for kosher cooks, because they don't have kosher certification, but any kosher chocolate cookie may serve as a substitute.

For baked cheesecakes, we also prefer sweet chocolate, which doesn't mean that the chocolate contains loads of sugar. It merely means that it contains a higher ratio of cocoa and is thus more deliciously dense. Our favorite is Maillard's Eagle Sweet Chocolate, but we also find Baker's quite acceptable, and it's easier to procure.

Don't look for bargains in cream cheese. The fewer the additives, the better the flavor. We've tried many of the no-frills store-label brands, and we generally find them mushy and gummy. We've been very satisfied with the Philadelphia Brand Cream cheese (which, by the way, has no history in Philly, though we like to say that Mother Wonderful is Philadelphia Brand Myra Chanin). You can see the difference in quality as soon as you remove the foil wrapper. The block of good cream cheese keeps its shape.

The high road to imaginative cheesecakes is paved with flavorings and extracts. We're always on the lookout for them, no matter where we may be. Most people leave Harrods in London with adornments for their bodies. Myra ignored all the marked-down fashions on sale the day after Christmas and walked out with an entire line of extracts which she'd never seen anywhere else. In the States, McCormick natural flavors and extracts come in vanilla, almond, anise, lemon, orange, peppermint, pineapple, and sherry, and are available in 1-ounce bottles at most supermarkets for a nominal price. Wagner extracts in adorable little 1½-ounce bottles include almond, anise, banana, black walnut, butter, rum butter, butterscotch, caramel, cherry, chocolate, cinnamon, ginger, lemon, lime, maple, mocha, orange, peppermint, pineapple, raspberry, rum, spearmint, strawberry, and wintergreen for about $2–$3 per bottle in gourmet and specialty food shops. The most exotic may be the La Torre extracts, which are artificial but artful flavors. Even though they were designed as cordial and liqueur flavorings, they blend perfectly into cheesecake batter. Because they are artificial flavors, even a recovering alcoholic can use them with no fear. La Torre flavors include cinnamon, peach, almond, cherry, peach brandy, amaretto, cherry brandy, pineapple, cognac, raspberry, anise, crema di cacao, rock and rye, anisette, crema di menta, apricot, curaçao, Jamaica rum, apricot brandy, Galliano, rum, brandy, banana, gin, rye, B&B, Sambuca, Benedictine, Grand Marnier, blackberry, Kaiser pear, strawberry, blackberry brandy, kirsch, Strega, bourbon, lemon, tutti-frutti, vermouth, Chartreuse, marsala, whiskey, cherry, and orange. They're priced at around $1.40 per ounce bottle and are available by mail from the Spice Corner, 904 South Ninth Street, Philadelphia, PA 19147.

Another great source for nut and fruit flavorings and syrups is the Cook's Wares catalog (www.cookswares.com) which carries both Monin's brand nut and fruit syrups and Cook's brand flavorings and extracts.

Made in France since 1912, Monin syrups are highly concentrated, certified kosher, made entirely from natural fruits and nut essences and white beet sugar, and contain no preservatives.

Monin's flavors include almond, caramel, cherry, cranberry, hazelnut, Irish cream, kiwi, mango, raspberry, strawberry, Swiss chocolate at $5.30 per 8½-ounce bottle, and all of the above plus anise, apple, apricot, black currant, blackberry, blue curaçao, blueberry, chocolate mint, cinnamon, coconut, coffee, frosted mint, gin, ginger, grapefruit, green banana, green mint, grenadine, honey, jasmine, lemon, lime, lychee, mandarin, melon, orange, passion fruit, peach, pear, pineapple, pistachio, rum, triple sec, vanilla, and yellow banana in 25-ounce bottles for $11.

A Cook's Wares catalog also offers Cook's brand flavorings and extracts, made with no additives, sweeteners, or coloring. Cook's line includes anise, blackberry, bourbon, brandy, chocolate, cinnamon, hazelnut, Java Crème, Pure Lemon, Pure Lime, Pure Maple, Pure Orange, Peppermint, Red Raspberry, Pure Rum, and Pure Strawberry in 2-ounce bottles for $6.00.

Another excellent source of flavoring is found in a collection of Boyajian's 5-ounce bottles of pure citrus oils which are naturally cold pressed from the rind of fresh fruit and retail for between $6 and $14 as follows: orange ($6), lemon ($12), lime ($11), tangerine ($14), and grapefruit ($8). These citrus oils are very potent and intense. It takes about 220 oranges, 330 lemons, or 400 limes to produce a 5-ounce bottle of citrus oil. I suggest you start by adding 1½ teaspoons of any of these citrus oils to a batch of batter, then taste, and if you want a more intense flavor, add from ¼ to ½ teaspoon more.

Boyajian's natural flavorings (available in sets of three 1-ounce bottles for $9) come in the following combinations—strawberry, cherry, and raspberry; anise, clove, and cinnamon; peppermint, spearmint, and wintergreen.

With these flavorings, syrups, and extracts, you can make any cheesecake that's in this book!

MEASUREMENTS

$\mathcal{T}$o help you figure out how much of what you'll need to make one cup of crumbs, here are some meaningful measurements we've made. We do recommend getting a small kitchen scale because we think its weight determinations are more consistent. You don't need a state-of-the-art wonder that tallies how many calories you swallowed while no one was looking. A small kitchen scale is adequate and will do the trick—the kind that people who claim to be on diets use to measure the amounts they hope they'll be eating.

NUMBER OF COOKIES REQUIRED TO PRODUCE ONE CUP OF CRUMBS		
TYPE OF COOKIE	COARSELY CHOPPED	FINELY CHOPPED
Chips Ahoy	8 cookies	11 cookies
Chocolate wafers	14 cookies	18 cookies
Graham crackers	10 crackers	14 crackers
Shortbread	13 cookies	14 cookies
Vanilla wafers	20 cookies	25 cookies
Gingersnaps	12 cookies	18 cookies
Chocolate sandwich	9 cookies	13 cookies

More Than You Ever Wanted to Know About Nuts

For crusts, we prefer nuts chopped medium fine—somewhere between small chunks and nut butter. Ideal nut bits should be the size of kosher salt, and fine but fluffy.

Never Chop Nuts in Advance
and Store Them!

You want them as fresh as possible so they don't get oily—even rancid—and make your crust too greasy when they combine with the other ingredients. You can start with either whole nuts or nut pieces/chunks in your processor. Run it for 20 seconds and then continue chopping using the on-off pulse—checking the texture of the nuts every 15 or 20 pulses, as well as stirring them around to keep their texture consistent; otherwise, some of them will turn into nut butter. Hard nuts like almonds acquire the desired texture easily. Softer nuts like macadamia and pine nuts have to be closely watched or they will mush up.

The following nut chart is direct from the horse's mouth—Planters', but slightly corrected. Since so many people end up buying those little packets found on supermarket racks, these measurements will help you buy just the amount that you need. Don't pay any attention to the measurements on the outside of the package. We've reweighed and remeasured them and gotten quite different results. We don't know what kind of measuring equipment Planters uses, but ours come directly from the "Nothing Above 99 Cents" store. We kept all the measurements in 2-ounce portions, so they'd be consistent.

BAGGED 2-OUNCE PACKAGES OF NUTS

TYPE OF NUT	CHOPPED MEDIUM FINE
ALMONDS	
Blanched, slivered	½ cup + 1 tablespoon
Blanched, whole	½ cup + 2 tablespoons
Sliced, with skin	½ cup
Whole, with skin	½ cup
BRAZIL NUTS	
Whole	½ cup + 1 tablespoon.
CASHEWS	
Pieces	½ cup
HAZELNUTS (FILBERTS)	
Whole, with skin	½ cup + 1 tablespoon
PEANUTS	
Whole, without skin	½ cup + 2 tablespoons
PECANS	
Pieces	½ cup + 1 tablespoon
MACADAMIAS	
Whole	½ cup scant
PINE NUTS	
Whole, without skin	½ cup
PISTACHIOS	
Whole	½ cup + 1 tablespoon
WALNUTS	
Black, pieces	½ cup scant
English, pieces	½ cup

Here's another nut table we designed to be used as a rule of thumb for readers like us who are overwhelmed by fractions:

1 ounce nut meats = ¼ cup chopped nuts
2 ounces nut meats = ½ cup chopped nuts
3 ounces nut meats = ¾ cup chopped nuts
4 ounces nut meats = 1 cup chopped nuts

Weigh them, chop them and then measure them. If you're short, you can always grind a few more. Just be warned that 1 ounce of overchopped nuts gives you 2 tablespoons of nut butter, so if you have to choose the lesser of two evils, underchop rather than overchop. Chopping the nuts in your food processor along with your cookie crumbs will prevent the nuts from turning mushy because the cookie crumbs will absorb the excess oil.

Twenty-Three Tips for
Making Perfectly Baked
Cheesecakes Every Time

READ BEFORE BAKING!!!!

1. Think Positive

Stay out of the kitchen when you're feeling guilty or distracted. Your cakes will end up either raw or burned. You'll gain fifteen pounds while making them—from nibbling on the ingredients. You'll scald and cut yourself and end up covered with bandages from clavicle to wrist. Never bake when you're feeling depressed. Take to your bed with a trashy book or meet someone amusing for lunch. Even better, take to your bed with a trashy man or woman who's amusing; but if you knew someone trashy and amusing, you probably wouldn't be feeling depressed.

2. Pardon Our Redundancies

We've always hated cookbooks that are designed for the convenience of the author, with instructions that make you shift from the page you're working on to a different section of the book that contains some important information for some part of the cake. We write for flawed folks, like ourselves, with short attention spans, imperfect vision, and faulty memories, who *hate* flipping through cookbooks searching for parts of recipes (like ingredients for a crumb crust) that were included only in a preceding chapter.

Each recipe has every pertinent bit of information and almost every applicable tip. However, we do run on and offer nitty-gritty advice on procedures that really do not need to be included over and over. These extensive explanations of procedures are usually covered in these tips, and we suggest that you read them to determine if the detailed instructions will be useful to you.

3. Do Not Worry About Running Short of Crumb-Crust Mix

If you run out of crumb-crust mix before you have covered your entire springform pan bottom, either flatten the mix you've pressed against the side of the pan and use that on the bottom, or just use some plain cookie crumbs or chopped nuts to fill the empty spots.

4. Use Plastic-Wrap Mittens to Press Down the Crumb-Crust Mix Around the Pan

The easiest and best way to spread the crumb-crust mix around a springform pan is to cover the fingers of your pressing hand with plastic wrap. This keeps the grease off your hands and in the mix, where it belongs.

5. Never Bake Cheesecakes at the Last Minute

Cheesecakes should be baked about two days before serving and allowed to mellow in the refrigerator. They will keep for at least a week refrigerated and several months frozen.

6. Use Professional Equipment

Throwaway aluminum containers are a no-no! They simply don't conduct heat properly.

In our recipes, when we say a mixer, we mean a mixer with a bowl that stays stationary and beaters that move. A little hand mixer just doesn't do a good enough job whipping up cream cheese, and it won't incorporate the eggs quickly enough. Good equipment costs more, but it does more and lasts longer. The right mixer will make whipping egg whites a snap and folding them into batter a dream instead of a nightmare. We've been using the same KitchenAid mixers for fifteen years and have never had a single problem with any of them. Buy a KitchenAid mixer and a good food processor, and stop struggling with cheap appliances.

7. In the Beginning, Follow These Recipes Exactly

Cooking is an art, but baking is a science. To be on the safe side, do like we tell ya. These recipes have been tested, retested, and re-retested.

8. Always Check Out and Measure Out Your Ingredients Before You Begin to Bake

Never assume you have every ingredient that you'll need. Make sure you do before you start to make a cake.

There is nothing more detrimental to excellent baking than finding that you don't have enough—or any—of an essential ingredient when you're at a crucial preparation point. It makes you crazy, and you hysterically start looking for ways to replace whatever's missing—and you usually can't. If you haven't begun to mix, you can always stop what you're doing, without wasting anything, or you can simply switch to another recipe for which you have all the ingredients. When working with a recipe you've never tried before, it's also helpful to measure out all the ingredients. That lets you concentrate totally on the cooking process without any anxiety.

9. Never Add Extracts to Unadulterated Melted Chocolate

Chocolate and alcohol don't go well together. Extracts will harden both white and dark chocolate. You must either blend the chocolate with melted butter, or add it to the batter before adding extracts or liqueur.

10. Check Your Oven's Temperature with a Thermometer to Ascertain That What You Want Is What You Get

An incorrect oven temperature always produces inconsistent results or absolute disasters. So make sure the heat in the oven is exactly what the recipe specifies.

11. Do Not Cheat on Ingredients

Never cut corners on ingredients in the name of economy. It ain't thrifty to throw out an entire cake because it tastes awful and nobody will eat it. The cost differential between a sublime cheesecake and a fourth-rate one is less than three dollars. If money is a problem, serve smaller slices, but always make sure anyone who tastes it will rave about your skill and beg for more.

Use the highest-quality cheese, eggs, sour cream, and liqueurs available in your area. Find a dried-fruit-and-nut emporium that does a huge business.

Their merchandise is always fresh. Or patronize a gourmet shop owned by a food fetishist who'd rather die than sell anything that isn't top drawer. (Of course, he/she may not be in business for very long.)

We can afford to purchase first-class ingredients because we never buy clothing with someone else's monogram on it, lest we begin to think we really are Gloria Montana or Ralph von Gucci and can't understand why Donald Trump doesn't invite *us* to his parties and charity balls. We're always amused by a lawyer we know who fancies himself a gourmet, but complains about the outrageous price of imported chocolate, while driving around town in his latest Rolls-Royce.

12. Always Add Eggs to Your Batter with Your Mixer on the Lowest Speed

When your mixer is set on high speed, too much air gets into the batter, and produces an inferior consistency, along with cheesecakes that develop depressions in the middle. Then you need to put a bunch of cornstarchy gunk on top to hide the hole. Yuck!

13. Let Your Cheesecake Nap Briefly Before You Glaze It

It is vital that the baked batter rest in the pan on the countertop for ten minutes after the initial baking and before you apply the sour-cream glaze. This very essential step allows the batter to solidify. Also, if there are any cracks in the cake, they'll appear then, so you can cover them with the sour-cream glaze.

14. Never Let Your Cheesecake Cool at Room Temperature

Despite anything you may have heard to the contrary from anyone, unless you run your cake directly from the oven to the refrigerator, your cheesecake will develop cracks and fissures and look awful.

15. Never Cover Your Cheesecake with Aluminum Foil or Plastic Wrap While It's in Your Fridge

If you do, condensation will cause a lake to form on top of the cake. Leave it in the pan uncovered until it cools down, and then put a cardboard round on it that will absorb moisture. Once cheesecakes have cooled, you can put them in a covered box, or just keep the cardboard round on top of the ring to protect the cake.

16. Do Not Serve Your Cheesecake Directly from Your Refrigerator

Always allow the cake to sit at room temperature for an hour or two before serving to enhance the flavor. Cheesecake is most sensuous when it's not too cold. If you're in a hurry to serve, let it sit at room temperature for at least 10 minutes, to give the butter in the crust a chance to relax its bond with the metal rim.

17. Never Even Think About Using Those Gunky Cornstarch Fruit Toppings on Any of Our Cheesecakes

Lest the Butterfat Fairy herself steal into your kitchen to dump salt in your sugar bowl. We hate those gunky cornstarch-and-fruit toppings. They remind us of the tinted plaster of paris sushi you see in the windows of Japanese restaurants—the ones we normally avoid. Gunky toppings were designed to conceal major imperfections in OPCs—Other People's Cheesecakes—like crevasses and hollows usually caused by incorrect temperature and too long a stay in the oven. OPCs are also beset with two other culinary blights: banal and boring lemon-flavored batter and/or soggy graham-cracker crumb crusts. We can't decide which one of the above constitutes the greatest gastronomical transgression. In our cheesecakes, the cookie crusts are crunchy, the batters are full-flavored and unique. If you follow our instructions, none of them will have any cracks on top that need to be filled in and disguised. An enticingly flavored sour-cream glaze—never all vanilla, it turns yellow—adds a mysterious tang and supplies a prime veneer.

18. Never Defile Your Crusts with Graham-Cracker Crumbs

Why? Don't even ask. They're way too soggy.

19. Use Your Imagination

Don't be afraid to experiment. If the results aren't perfect, don't worry. As long as it's sweet, somebody in your household will devour it. If an ingredient intrigues you, go for it, and try to develop flavors of your own. If you make an outstanding one, send us the recipe, and we'll give you a credit in our next cheesecake cookbook.

20. Does the Liqueur Used to Flavor These Cheesecakes Present Any Problem to Recovering Alcoholics?

Not in the least. The amounts used are minuscule, and the alcohol burns off during the baking process. However, if you are concerned, you can simply replace the liqueurs or brandy with artificial extracts or natural flavorings.

21. What Do You Do If You Wish to Make a Smaller Cheesecake?

You can make a half-size version of any one of these baked cheesecakes by using an 8-inch springform pan with only a half-portion of each ingredient, and by baking the batter for only 40 minutes. Everything else—including the time for baking the glaze—remains the same.

22. What If You Find That
Seasonal Fruits Are Out of Season?

Not to worry. Now that we're importing fruits from South America and New
Zealand, you'll find that every fruit created by God is in season somewhere in
the world. To get them, you simply have to rub your greengrocer with money.

23. What About Dietary
Restrictions for Observing Jews?

If you're an observant Jew who keeps a kosher kitchen, every one of the ingredients in these recipes is available in a kosher certified form.

BAKED CHEESECAKE RECIPES

Basic Lime-Almond Cheesecake

Preheat oven to 350 degrees F. If ingredients are not at room temperature, add five minutes to baking time.

CRUST

¼ pound (1 stick) lightly salted butter

2 cups finely ground vanilla-wafer crumbs

¼ cup sugar

Melt butter over very low heat. Combine butter with crumbs and sugar in a food processor until thoroughly blended or stir and mash together with a fork in a roomy bowl. Press small amounts of crust mix bit by bit all the way up the sides of an ungreased 10″ springform pan first, and then press over the bottom of the pan.

BATTER

2	pounds (4 8-ounce packages) cream cheese
1½	cups sugar
1½	tablespoons lime juice
	pinch of salt
4	large eggs

In a mixer, whip cream cheese on the highest speed for 5 minutes, then add sugar and whip for 2 minutes more. Add lime juice and salt and blend together thoroughly. Add the eggs, one at a time, keeping the mixer on the lowest speed in order to prevent too much air from destroying the proper consistency of the batter; mix just until each egg has been incorporated into the batter.

NOTE: If you use a food processor to prepare the batter, blend well and add the eggs one at a time until they are just incorporated into the batter.

Pour batter into the crust and bake in a preheated oven for 50–55 minutes. Remove cake from oven—but do not turn oven off—and let stand on a countertop for 10 minutes while you prepare sour-cream glaze. This essential step allows the interior of the cake to solidify without overbaking or burning. Any cracks in the cake will be concealed under the sour-cream glaze.

SOUR-CREAM GLAZE

2	cups sour cream
¼	cup sugar
1	teaspoon almond extract

Combine sour cream, sugar, and extract with a rubber spatula in a bowl. Do not use a mixer unless it is on a very low speed. Spread evenly and smoothly over top of baked filling and return to 350 degree F. oven for 10 minutes. Remove from oven and place **immediately** in refrigerator to cool. This prevents cracks from forming on top of the cake.

Before serving, let cheesecake stand at room temperature for 10 minutes to allow the butter in the crust to loosen its bond with the metal ring. When you release the springform clasp, the crust will generally detach naturally from the sides. If it sticks, separate crust from the sides gently with a metal spatula or a sharp knife.

Triple Chocolate Cheesecake

Preheat oven to 350 degrees F. If ingredients are not at room temperature, add five minutes to baking time.

CRUST

¼ pound (1 stick) lightly salted butter

2 cups finely ground chocolate-cookie crumbs

¼ cup sugar

Melt butter over very low heat. Combine butter with crumbs and sugar in a food processor until thoroughly blended or stir and mash together with a fork in a roomy bowl. Press small amounts of crust mix bit by bit all the way up the sides of an ungreased 10″ springform pan first, and then press remaining crust mix on the bottom of the pan.

BATTER

4 ounces sweet chocolate

2 pounds (4 8-ounce packages) cream cheese

1½ cups sugar

1 tablespoon dark Jamaican rum

1 teaspoon vanilla extract

   pinch of salt

4 large eggs

½ cup chocolate chips

Melt sweet chocolate in the top of a double boiler, or in a microwave oven at half power, and reserve.

In a mixer, whip cream cheese on the highest speed for 5 minutes, then add sugar and whip for 2 minutes more. Add melted chocolate, rum, vanilla, and salt and blend together thoroughly. Add the eggs, one at a time, keeping the mixer on the lowest speed in order to prevent too much air from destroying the proper consistency of the batter; mix just until each egg has been incorporated into the batter. Stir in chocolate chips.

NOTE: If you use a food processor to prepare the batter, blend the ingredients well and add the eggs one at a time until they are just incorporated into the batter.

Pour batter into the crust and bake in a preheated oven for 40–45 minutes. Remove cake from oven and let stand on a countertop for 10 minutes while you prepare sour-cream glaze. This essential step allows the interior of the cake to solidify without overbaking or burning. Any cracks in the cake will be concealed under the sour-cream glaze.

SOUR-CREAM GLAZE
- 2 cups sour cream
- ¼ cup sugar
- 1 teaspoon almond extract
- shaved chocolate

Combine sour cream, sugar, and almond extract with a rubber spatula in a plastic bowl. Spread evenly and smoothly over top of baked filling and return to 350 degree F. oven for 10 minutes. Remove from oven, sprinkle glaze with shaved chocolate, and place **immediately** in refrigerator to cool. This prevents cracks from forming on top of the cake.

Before serving, let cheesecake stand at room temperature for 10 minutes to allow the butter in the crust to loosen its bond with the metal ring. When you release the springform clasp, the crust will generally detach naturally from the sides. If it sticks, separate crust from the sides gently with a metal spatula or a sharp knife.

Joey's Best-Selling Bloomingdale's
Key Lime Cheesecake

Preheat oven to 300 degrees F.

CRUST

2 cups finely ground vanilla-wafer crumbs

1 cup Florida crystal, turbinado, or date sugar

¼ pound pecans

1 teaspoon ground cinnamon

¼ pound lightly salted butter, melted

Process graham crackers, sugar, pecans, cinnamon, and butter in a food processor until finely ground and well combined. Press around the bottom and sides of a 10-inch springform pan.

BATTER

2 pounds (4 8-ounce packages) cream cheese,
     at room temperature

1 cup sugar

   juice from one fresh Key lime

   pinch of salt

4 large eggs

Combine cream cheese, sugar, lime juice, and salt in a bowl, mixer, or food processor. Add the eggs, one at a time, and blend at a low speed until batter is creamy. Pour batter into crust. Put a pan of water in the lower third of the oven. Put the cheesecake above the pan of water in the lower half of the oven and bake for 1 hour. Remove cheesecake from oven and let cool for 15 minutes, but keep the oven on because you'll be using it for the topping.

TOPPING

1 cup sour cream

¼ cup sugar

1 tablespoon almond extract

Mix together sour cream, sugar, and almond extract. Spread over baked cake and bake for 15 minutes more. Remove from oven and refrigerate overnight before serving.

Joey's Mango Cheesecake

Preheat oven to 350 degrees F.

CRUST

½ cup cake flour

1 teaspoon baking powder

pinch of salt

4 large eggs, separated

½ cup Florida crystal or turbinado sugar

¼ teaspoon vanilla extract

¼ teaspoon fresh lime juice

4 tablespoons lightly salted butter, melted

⅛ teaspoon cream of tartar

Butter a 10-inch springform pan. Combine flour, baking powder, and salt in a bowl and reserve. Beat egg yolks in a mixer on high speed for 2 minutes. Add ⅓ cup sugar, vanilla, and lime juice and beat for 3 minutes more. Add reserved flour and stir until well combined. Mix in butter and reserve.

In another bowl, whip the egg whites with cream of tartar until soft peaks form. Add the remaining sugar one tablespoon at a time and whip until the sugar and egg whites are well combined. Fold the egg whites into the reserved batter and spoon into pan. Bake for 8 minutes, or until the crust springs back.

BATTER

2 pounds (4 8-ounce packages) cream cheese

1 cup Florida crystal or turbinado sugar

1 mango, peeled, pitted and pureed

1 tablespoon fresh lime juice

pinch of salt

4 large eggs

In a mixing bowl, beat cream cheese and sugar together. Add mango, lime juice, and salt and combine. Add the eggs, one at a time, beating until batter is creamy, then pour the batter into the baked crust. Bake for 45 minutes. Let it cool overnight in the fridge before serving.

Joey's Pareve Vegan Tofu Cheesecake

Preheat oven to 300 degrees F.

CRUST

¼ cup pecans

2 cups finely ground vanilla-wafer crumbs

¼ cup dry malt sweetener

⅛ teaspoon cinnamon

1 stick soy margarine, melted

In a food processor, finely chop together pecans, graham crackers, malt sweetener, and cinnamon. Add margarine and blend well. Line the bottom and sides of a 10-inch springform pan with crust mix.

BATTER

3 pounds (4 12-ounce or 3 16-ounce packages) silken tofu

1 cup malt sweetener or maple syrup

juice of 1 lime

pinch of salt

egg substitute equivalent to 4 eggs

Beat tofu, sweetener, lime juice, salt, and egg substitute for 2 minutes. Pour into crust. Put a pan of water in the lower third of the oven. Put the cheesecake above the pan of water in the lower half of the oven and bake for 1 hour. Remove oven and let cool for 15 minutes, but keep the oven hot because you'll be using it again.

TOPPING

1 pint nondairy sour cream substitute

4 tablespoons malt sweetener

½ teaspoon almond extract

Combine sour cream, malt sweetener, and extract, spread over top of cake and bake for 15 minutes longer. Refrigerate overnight before serving.

Grand Caramel Nut Cheesecake

Preheat oven to 350 degrees F. If ingredients are not at room temperature, add five minutes to baking time.

CRUST

¼ pound (1 stick) lightly salted butter

1 cup finely ground vanilla-wafer crumbs

1 cup finely chopped pecans

¼ cup brown sugar, firmly packed

Melt butter over very low heat. Combine butter with crumbs, nuts, and sugar in a food processor until thoroughly blended, or stir and mash together with a fork in a roomy bowl. Press small amounts of crust mix bit by bit all the way up the sides of an ungreased 10″ springform pan first and then press over the bottom of the pan.

BATTER

2 pounds (4 8-ounce packages) cream cheese

1½ cups white sugar

1½ tablespoons Grand Marnier liqueur

½ cup pecan or cashew brittle, chopped

pinch of salt

4 large eggs

⅓ cup caramel-flavored topping

1 teaspoon caramel flavoring

In a mixer whip cream cheese on the highest speed for 5 minutes, then add sugar and whip for 2 minutes more. Add liqueur, brittle, and salt and blend together well. Add the eggs, one at a time, keeping the mixer on the lowest speed to prevent too much air from destroying the proper consistency of the batter; mix just until each egg has been incorporated.

Remove one cup of batter and reserve. Pour remainder into the crust. Add caramel topping and flavoring to the reserved batter and blend well with a spoon or spatula. Pour the caramel batter into the center of the pan, and cut through several times with a knife to achieve a swirl effect. Bake in a pre-heated oven for 45–50 minutes. Remove cake from oven and let stand on a countertop for 10 minutes while you prepare sour cream glaze. This essential step allows the interior of the cake to solidify without overbaking or burning. Any cracks in the cake will be concealed under the sour-cream glaze.

SOUR-CREAM GLAZE

- 2 cups sour cream
- ¼ cup sugar
- 1 teaspoon Grand Marnier
- ½ cup pecan or cashew brittle, chopped

Combine sour cream, sugar, and Grand Marnier with a rubber spatula in a plastic bowl. Spread evenly and smoothly over top of baked filling, sprinkle with brittle and return to 350 degree F. oven for 10 minutes. Remove from oven and place **immediately** in refrigerator to cool. This prevents cracks from forming on top of the glaze.

Before serving, let cheesecake stand at room temperature for 10 minutes to allow the butter in the crust to loosen its bond with the metal ring. When you release the springform clasp, the crust will generally detach naturally from the sides. If it sticks, separate crust from the sides gently with a metal spatula or a sharp knife.

Ginger Pear Cheesecake

Preheat oven to 350 degrees F. If ingredients are not at room temperature, add five minutes to baking time.

PRELIMINARY

2 dried pear halves

3 tablespoons fine cognac

Cut pears into slivers and soak in cognac. When ready to make batter, drain and reserve pears and cognac separately.

CRUST

¼ pound (1 stick) lightly salted butter

1 cup finely ground gingersnap crumbs

1 cup finely ground vanilla-wafer crumbs

¼ cup sugar

Melt butter over very low heat. Combine butter with crumbs and sugar in a food processor until thoroughly blended or stir and mash together with a fork in a roomy bowl. Press small amounts of crust mix bit by bit all the way up the sides of an ungreased 10″ springform pan first, and then press over bottom of the pan.

BATTER

2 pounds (4 8-ounce packages) cream cheese

1½ cups sugar

1½ tablespoons reserved cognac

½ teaspoon vanilla extract

pinch of salt

4 large eggs

reserved slivered cognac-soaked pears

2 chunks crystallized ginger

In a mixer, whip cream cheese on the highest speed for 5 minutes, then add sugar and whip for 2 minutes more. Add reserved cognac, vanilla, salt, and blend together thoroughly. Add the eggs, one at a time, keeping the mixer on the lowest speed in order to prevent too much air from destroying the proper consistency of the batter; mix just until each egg has been incorporated into the batter. Slice ginger very thin and fold ginger and slivered pears into batter with a rubber spatula to prevent them from sinking to the bottom. Pour batter into crust and bake in preheated oven for 55–60 minutes.

Remove from oven and let stand on a countertop for 10 minutes while you prepare sour-cream glaze. This essential step allows the interior of the cake to solidify without overbaking or burning. Any cracks in the cake will be concealed under the sour-cream glaze.

SOUR-CREAM GLAZE

- 2 cups sour cream
- ¼ cup sugar
- ½ teaspoon reserved cognac
- ½ teaspoon vanilla extract
- 4 drops of ginger extract or liqueur
- 1 chunk crystallized ginger

Combine sour cream, sugar, cognac, and extracts with a rubber spatula in a plastic bowl. Spread evenly and smoothly over top of baked filling. Slice ginger into 12 slivers and arrange them vertically around the rim of sour-cream glaze like numbers on a clock face. Return cake to 350 degree F. oven for 10 minutes. Remove from oven and place immediately in refrigerator to cool. This prevents cracks from forming in the cake.

Before serving, let the cheesecake stand at room temperature for 10 minutes to allow the butter in the crust to loosen its bond with the metal ring. When you release the springform clasp, the crust will generally detach naturally from the sides. If it sticks, separate crust from the sides gently with a metal spatula or a sharp knife.

Honey Fig Cheesecake

Preheat oven to 350 degrees F. If ingredients are not at room temperature, add five minutes to baking time.

CRUST

¼ pound (1 stick) lightly salted butter

2 cups finely ground vanilla-wafer crumbs

¼ cup sugar

Melt butter over very low heat. Combine butter with crumbs and sugar in a food processor until thoroughly blended or stir and mash together with a fork in a roomy bowl. Press small amounts of crust mix bit by bit all the way up the sides of an ungreased 10″ springform pan first, and then press over the bottom of the pan.

BATTER

2 pounds (4 8-ounce packages) cream cheese

1 cup sugar

1 teaspoon rose-petal water*

1 teaspoon orange-flower water

1 teaspoon lemon juice

¼ cup honey

   pinch salt

4 large eggs

4 dried figs, cut into long strips

In a mixer, whip cream cheese on the highest speed for 5 minutes, then add sugar and whip for 2 minutes more. Add rose-petal water, orange-flower water, lemon juice, honey, and salt and blend together thoroughly. Add the eggs, one at a time, keeping the mixer on the lowest speed in order to pre-

*Rose-petal water and orange-flower water may be found in Greek or Middle Eastern groceries. There is no substitute for them. They give the cake a very sensuous flavor. If they are unavailable in your town, order them from the Spice Corner in Philadelphia (215-925-1660).

vent too much air from destroying the proper consistency of the batter; mix just until each egg has been incorporated into the batter. Fold in figs.

Pour batter into the crust and bake in a preheated oven for 50–55 minutes. Remove cake from oven and let stand on a countertop for 10 minutes while you prepare sour-cream glaze. This essential step allows the interior of the cake to solidify without overbaking or burning. Any cracks in the cake will be concealed under the sour-cream glaze.

SOUR-CREAM GLAZE

2 cups sour cream

¼ cup sugar

1 teaspoon almond extract

2 figs, cut into long thin strips (12 slices)

½ cup chopped walnuts

Combine sour cream, sugar, and extract with a rubber spatula in a plastic bowl. Spread evenly and smoothly over top of baked filling and return to 350 degree F. oven for 10 minutes. Remove from oven, place fig strips on the cake like the numbers on a clock face, sprinkle with walnuts, and place **immediately** in refrigerator to cool. This prevents cracks from forming on top of the glaze.

Before serving, let cheesecake stand at room temperature for 10 minutes to allow the butter in the crust to loosen its bond with the metal ring. When you release the springform clasp, the crust will generally detach naturally from the sides. If it sticks, separate crust from the sides gently with a metal spatula or a sharp knife.

AN OPTIONAL BUT SENSATIONAL
ADDED GARNISH

1 cup honey

1 cup sugar

2 cups water

1 teaspoon lemon juice

1 teaspoon rose-petal water

1 teaspoon orange-flower water

Combine all the above ingredients in a pan, bring to a boil and then simmer for 20 minutes until the syrup thickens. Dribble 3 tablespoons of the syrup over the top of the cake 2 hours before serving. Refrigerate the remainder and then reheat it in a microwave when you make another Honey Fig Cheesecake or use it as a topping on ice cream or fruit.

Banana Daiquiri Cheesecake

Preheat oven to 350 degrees F. If ingredients are not at room temperature, add five minutes to baking time.

CRUST

¼ pound (1 stick) lightly salted butter

2 cups finely ground vanilla-wafer crumbs

¼ cup sugar

Melt butter over very low heat. Combine butter with crumbs and sugar in a food processor until thoroughly blended or stir and mash together with a fork in a roomy bowl. Press small amounts of crust mix bit by bit all the way up the sides of an ungreased 10″ springform pan first, and then press over the bottom of the pan.

BATTER

2 pounds (4 8-ounce packages) cream cheese

1½ cups sugar

5 teaspoons banana extract or liqueur

1 teaspoon dark rum

1 teaspoon lime juice

½ ripe, almost mushy banana, mashed

pinch of salt

4 large eggs

1½ ripe bananas, sliced very thin

In a mixer, whip cream cheese on the highest speed for 5 minutes, then add sugar and whip for 2 minutes more. Add extract or liqueur, rum, lime juice, mashed banana, and salt and blend together thoroughly. Add the eggs, one at a time, keeping the mixer on the lowest speed in order to prevent too much air from destroying the proper consistency of the batter; mix just until each egg has been incorporated into the batter.

Pour half of the batter into the crust and arrange the sliced bananas vertically into the batter. Pour remaining batter on top and bake in a preheated oven for 55–60 minutes. Remove cake from oven and let stand on a counter-top for 10 minutes while you prepare sour-cream glaze. This essential step allows the interior of the cake to solidify without overbaking or burning. Any cracks in the cake will be concealed under the sour-cream glaze.

SOUR-CREAM GLAZE

- 2 cups sour cream
- ¼ cup sugar
- 1 teaspoon coconut extract
- ½ cup coconut flakes

Combine sour cream, sugar, and extract with a rubber spatula in a plastic bowl. Spread evenly and smoothly over top of baked filling, sprinkle with coconut, and return to 350 degree F. oven for 10 minutes. Remove from oven and place **immediately** in refrigerator to cool. This prevents cracks from forming on top of the glaze.

Before serving, let cheesecake stand at room temperature for 10 minutes to allow the butter in the crust to loosen its bond with the metal ring. When you release the springform clasp, the crust will generally detach naturally from the sides. If it sticks, separate crust from the sides gently with a metal spatula or a sharp knife.

Piña Colada Cheesecake

Preheat oven to 350 degrees F. If ingredients are not at room temperature, add five minutes to baking time.

PRELIMINARY

2　round slices dried pineapple

3　tablespoons dark Jamaican rum

Cut pineapple into thin slivers and soak in rum. When ready to add to batter, drain and reserve rum and pineapple.

CRUST

¼　pound (1 stick) lightly salted butter

2　cups finely ground vanilla-wafer crumbs

¼　cup sugar

Melt butter over very low heat. Combine butter with crumbs and sugar in a food processor until thoroughly blended or stir and mash together with a fork in a roomy bowl. Press small amounts of crust mix bit by bit all the way up the sides of an ungreased 10″ springform pan first, and then press over the bottom of the pan.

BATTER

2　pounds (4 8-ounce packages) cream cheese

1½　cups sugar

2　teaspoons pineapple extract

1　tablespoon reserved dark rum

　　pinch of salt

4　large eggs

　　drained rum-soaked sliced pineapple

In a mixer, whip cream cheese on the highest speed for 5 minutes, then add sugar and whip for 2 minutes more. Add pineapple extract, rum, and salt and blend together thoroughly. Add the eggs, one at a time, keeping the mixer on the lowest speed in order to prevent too much air from destroying the proper consistency of the batter; mix just until each egg has been incorporated into the batter. Fold drained pineapple into the batter.

Pour batter into the crust and bake in a preheated oven for 50–55 minutes. Remove cake from oven and let stand on a countertop for 10 minutes while you prepare sour-cream glaze. This essential step allows the interior of the cake to solidify without overbaking or burning. Any cracks in the cake will be concealed under the sour-cream glaze.

SOUR-CREAM GLAZE

- 2 cups sour cream
- ¼ cup sugar
- 1 teaspoon coconut extract
- ½ cup coconut flakes

Combine sour cream, sugar, and extract with a rubber spatula in a plastic bowl. Spread evenly and smoothly over top of baked filling, sprinkle with coconut, and return to 350 degree F. oven for 10 minutes. Remove from oven and place **immediately** in refrigerator to cool. This prevents cracks from forming on top of the cake.

Before serving, let cheesecake stand at room temperature for 10 minutes to allow the butter in the crust to loosen its bond with the metal ring. When you release the springform clasp, the crust will generally detach naturally from the sides. If it sticks, separate crust from the sides gently with a metal spatula or a sharp knife.

Butternut Cheesecake

Preheat oven to 350 degrees F. If ingredients are not at room temperature, add five minutes to baking time.

CRUST
¼ pound (1 stick) lightly salted butter
2 cups finely ground vanilla-wafer crumbs
¼ cup sugar

Melt butter over very low heat. Combine butter with crumbs and sugar in a food processor until thoroughly blended or stir and mash together with a fork in a roomy bowl. Press small amounts of crust mix bit by bit all the way up the sides of an ungreased 10″ springform pan first, and then press over the bottom of the pan.

BATTER
6 ounces butterscotch bits
2 pounds (4 8-ounce packages) cream cheese
1¼ cups sugar
1½ tablespoons dark Jamaican rum
½ cup chopped pecans
   pinch salt
4 large eggs

Melt butterscotch bits over simmering water in the top of a double boiler, in a pan over simmering water, or in a microwave oven on half power, and reserve.

In a mixer, whip cream cheese on the highest speed for 5 minutes, then add sugar and whip for 2 minutes more. Add melted butterscotch bits, rum, pecans, and salt and blend together thoroughly. Add the eggs, one at a time, keeping the mixer on the lowest speed in order to prevent too much air from destroying the proper consistency of the batter; mix just until each egg has been incorporated into the batter.

Pour batter into the crust and bake in a preheated oven for 45–50 minutes.

Remove cake from oven and let stand on a countertop for 10 minutes while you prepare sour-cream glaze. This essential step allows the interior of the cake to solidify without overbaking or burning. Any cracks in the cake will be concealed under the sour-cream glaze.

SOUR-CREAM GLAZE

2 cups sour cream

¼ cup sugar

1 teaspoon rum

3 tablespoons chopped pecans

Combine sour cream, sugar, and extract with a rubber spatula in a plastic bowl. Spread evenly and smoothly over top of baked filling and return to 350 degree F. oven for 10 minutes. Remove from oven, sprinkle with nuts, and place **immediately** in refrigerator to cool. This prevents cracks from forming on top of the cake.

Before serving, let cheesecake stand at room temperature for 10 minutes to allow the butter in the crust to loosen its bond with the metal ring. When you release the springform clasp, the crust will generally detach naturally from the sides. If it sticks, separate crust from the sides gently with a metal spatula or a sharp knife.

Apricot Almond Cheesecake

Preheat oven to 350 degrees F. If ingredients are not at room temperature, add five minutes to baking time.

CRUST
¼ pound (1 stick) lightly salted butter

2 cups finely ground vanilla-wafer crumbs

¼ cup sugar

Melt butter over very low heat. Combine butter with crumbs and sugar in a food processor until thoroughly blended or stir and mash together with a fork in a roomy bowl. Press small amounts of crust mix bit by bit all the way up the sides of an ungreased 10″ springform pan first, and then press over the bottom of the pan.

BATTER
2 pounds (4 8-ounce packages) cream cheese

1½ cups sugar

½ teaspoon almond extract

1 teaspoon orange extract

1 tablespoon Grand Marnier

pinch of salt

4 large eggs

½ cup blanched, sliced almonds, lightly toasted

2 honey-glazed apricots, cut in half and sliced thinly

In a mixer, whip cream cheese on the highest speed for 5 minutes, then add sugar and whip for 2 minutes more. Add extracts, Grand Marnier, and salt and blend together thoroughly. Add the eggs, one at a time, keeping the mixer on the lowest speed in order to prevent too much air from destroying the proper consistency of the batter; mix just until each egg has been incorporated into the batter.

Pour one-third of the batter into the crust, sprinkle with half the almonds.

Top with a second layer of one-third of the batter. Insert apricot slices vertically into batter and sprinkle with remaining almonds. Smooth remaining batter on top and bake in a preheated oven for 50–55 minutes. Remove cake from oven and let stand on a countertop for 10 minutes while you prepare sour-cream glaze. This essential step allows the interior of the cake to solidify without overbaking or burning. Any cracks in the cake will be concealed under the sour-cream glaze.

SOUR-CREAM GLAZE

2 cups sour cream

¼ cup sugar

1 teaspoon almond extract

1 honey-glazed apricot cut into 12 thin slices

¼ cup blanched, sliced almonds, lightly toasted

Combine sour cream, sugar, and extract with a rubber spatula in a plastic bowl. Spread evenly and smoothly over top of baked filling, arrange apricot slices around the edge of the glaze like the numbers in a clock face, sprinkle with almonds, and return to 350 degree F. oven for 10 minutes. Remove from oven and place **immediately** in refrigerator to cool. This prevents cracks from forming on top of the cake.

Before serving, let cheesecake stand at room temperature for 10 minutes to allow the butter in the crust to loosen its bond with the metal ring. When you release the springform clasp, the crust will generally detach naturally from the sides. If it sticks, separate crust from the sides gently with a metal spatula or a sharp knife.

Chocolate Mint Cheesecake

Preheat oven to 350 degrees F. If ingredients are not at room temperature, add five minutes to baking time.

CRUST

¼   pound (1 stick) lightly salted butter

2   cups finely ground chocolate-cookie crumbs

¼   cup sugar

Melt butter over very low heat. Combine butter with crumbs and sugar in a food processor until thoroughly blended or stir and mash together with a fork in a roomy bowl. Press small amounts of crust mix bit by bit all the way up the sides of an ungreased 10″ springform pan first, and then press remaining crust mix on the bottom of the pan.

BATTER

4   ounces sweet chocolate

2   pounds (4 8-ounce packages) cream cheese

1½   cups sugar

1   tablespoon dark mint extract or liqueur

    pinch of salt

2   ounces mint-flavored chocolate, chopped, or

      mint-flavored chocolate chips

4   large eggs

Melt sweet chocolate in the top of a double boiler, or in a microwave oven at half power, and reserve.

In a mixer, whip cream cheese on the highest speed for 5 minutes, then add sugar and whip for 2 minutes more. Add melted chocolate, mint, and salt and blend together thoroughly. Add the eggs, one at a time, keeping the mixer on the lowest speed in order to prevent too much air from destroying the proper consistency of the batter; mix just until each egg has been incorporated into the batter. Stir in mint-flavored chocolate chips.

Pour batter into the crust and bake in a preheated oven for 40–45 minutes.

Remove cake from oven and let stand on a countertop for 10 minutes while you prepare sour-cream glaze. This essential step allows the interior of the cake to solidify without overbaking or burning. Any cracks in the cake will be concealed under the sour-cream glaze.

SOUR-CREAM GLAZE

- 2 cups sour cream
- ¼ cup sugar
- 1 teaspoon white crème de menthe
- fresh mint leaves

Combine sour cream, sugar, and crème de menthe with a rubber spatula in a plastic bowl. Spread evenly and smoothly over top of baked filling and return to 350 degree F. oven for 10 minutes. Remove from oven, sprinkle glaze with shaved chocolate, and place **immediately** in refrigerator to cool. This prevents cracks from forming on top of the cake.

Before serving, garnish with fresh mint leaves and let cheesecake stand at room temperature for 10 minutes to allow the butter in the crust to loosen its bond with the metal ring. When you release the springform clasp, the crust will generally detach naturally from the sides. If it sticks, separate crust from the sides gently with a metal spatula or a sharp knife.

Galliano Cheesecake

Preheat oven to 350 degrees F. If ingredients are not at room temperature, add five minutes to baking time.

CRUST

¼ pound (1 stick) lightly salted butter
2 cups finely ground arrowroot-biscuit crumbs
¼ cup sugar

Melt butter over very low heat. Combine butter with crumbs and sugar in a food processor until thoroughly blended or stir and mash together with a fork in a roomy bowl. Press small amounts of crust mix bit by bit all the way up the sides of an ungreased 10″ springform pan first, and then press over the bottom of the pan.

BATTER

2 pounds (4 8-ounce packages) cream cheese
1½ cups sugar
1 tablespoon Galliano liqueur
1 teaspoon orange extract
1 teaspoon almond extract
4 drops anisette flavoring
   pinch of salt
4 large eggs

In a mixer, whip cream cheese on the highest speed for 5 minutes, then add sugar and whip for 2 minutes more. Add Galliano, extracts, flavoring, and salt and blend together thoroughly. Add the eggs, one at a time, keeping the mixer on the lowest speed in order to prevent too much air from destroying the proper consistency of the batter; mix just until each egg has been incorporated into the batter.

Pour batter into the crust and bake in a preheated oven for 50–55 minutes. Remove cake from oven and let stand on a countertop for 10 minutes while you prepare sour-cream glaze. This essential step allows the interior of the

cake to solidify without overbaking or burning. Any cracks in the cake will be concealed under the sour-cream glaze.

SOUR-CREAM GLAZE
2 cups sour cream
¼ cup sugar
1 teaspoon almond extract

Combine sour cream, sugar, and extract with a rubber spatula in a plastic bowl. Spread evenly and smoothly over top of baked filling and return to 350 degree F. oven for 10 minutes. Remove from oven and place **immediately** in refrigerator to cool. This prevents cracks from forming on top of the cake.

Before serving, let cheesecake stand at room temperature for 10 minutes to allow the butter in the crust to loosen its bond with the metal ring. When you release the springform clasp, the crust will generally detach naturally from the sides. If it sticks, separate crust from the sides gently with a metal spatula or a sharp knife.

Maple Walnut Cheesecake

Preheat oven to 350 degrees F. If ingredients are not at room temperature, add five minutes to baking time.

CRUST
¼ pound (1 stick) lightly salted butter
½ cup finely chopped walnuts
1½ cups finely ground vanilla-wafer crumbs
¼ cup sugar

Melt butter over very low heat. Combine butter with nuts, crumbs, and sugar in a food processor until thoroughly blended or stir and mash together with a fork in a roomy bowl. Press small amounts of crust mix bit by bit all the way up the sides of an ungreased 10″ springform pan first, and then press over the bottom of the pan.

BATTER
2 pounds (4 8-ounce packages) cream cheese
1⅓ cups sugar
1 teaspoon maple extract
1 teaspoon vanilla extract
¼ cup maple syrup
pinch of salt
½ cup chopped walnuts
4 large eggs

In a mixer, whip cream cheese on the highest speed for 5 minutes, then add sugar and whip for 2 minutes more. Add extracts, maple syrup, salt, and walnuts and blend together thoroughly. Add the eggs, one at a time, keeping the mixer on the lowest speed in order to prevent too much air from destroying the proper consistency of the batter; mix just until each egg has been incorporated into the batter.

Pour batter into the crust and bake in a preheated oven for 45–50 minutes. Remove cake from oven and let stand on a countertop for 10 minutes while

you prepare sour-cream glaze. This essential step allows the interior of the cake to solidify without overbaking or burning. Any cracks in the cake will be concealed under the sour-cream glaze.

SOUR-CREAM GLAZE

2 cups sour cream

¼ cup sugar

1 teaspoon vanilla extract

¼ cup chopped walnuts

Combine sour cream, sugar, and extract with a rubber spatula in a plastic bowl. Spread evenly and smoothly over top of baked filling, sprinkle with nuts, and return to 350 degree F. oven for 10 minutes. Remove from oven and place **immediately** in refrigerator to cool. This prevents cracks from forming on top of the cake.

Before serving, let cheesecake stand at room temperature for 10 minutes to allow the butter in the crust to loosen its bond with the metal ring. When you release the springform clasp, the crust will generally detach naturally from the sides. If it sticks, separate crust from the sides gently with a metal spatula or a sharp knife.

Apricot Streusel Cheesecake

Preheat oven to 350 degrees F. If ingredients are not at room temperature, add five minutes to baking time.

PRELIMINARY

3½ tablespoons sugar
¼ cup chopped walnuts
½ teaspoon ground cinnamon

Mix streusel ingredients together in a bowl and reserve.

CRUST

¼ pound (1 stick) lightly salted butter
2 cups finely ground cinnamon-cookie crumbs
¼ cup sugar

Melt butter over very low heat. Combine butter with crumbs and sugar in a food processor until thoroughly blended or stir and mash together with a fork in a roomy bowl. Press small amounts of crust mix bit by bit all the way up the sides of an ungreased 10″ springform pan first, and then press over the bottom of the pan.

BATTER

2 pounds (4 8-ounce packages) cream cheese
1 cup sugar
1 tablespoon dark rum
1½ teaspoons vanilla extract
   pinch of salt
4 large eggs
½ cup apricot preserves
¼ teaspoon apricot brandy or brandy extract

In a mixer, whip cream cheese on the highest speed for 5 minutes, then add sugar and whip for 2 minutes more. Add rum, vanilla, and salt and blend together thoroughly. Add the eggs, one at a time, keeping the mixer on the lowest speed in order to prevent too much air from destroying the proper consistency of the batter; mix just until each egg has been incorporated into the batter.

Reserve one cup of batter and blend the apricot preserves and brandy flavoring into it. Reserve 2 tablespoons of the streusel topping to garnish the glaze.

Pour one-third of the remaining plain batter into the crust. Sprinkle with one-half of the unreserved streusel topping. Spread second layer of batter over nut mixture and sprinkle with the balance of the unreserved streusel topping. Cover with balance of plain batter. Pour apricot-flavored batter into the center of the cake and cut through several times with a knife to achieve a swirl effect. Bake in a preheated oven for 1 hour.

Remove cake from oven and let stand on a countertop for 10 minutes while you prepare sour-cream glaze. This essential step allows the interior of the cake to solidify without overbaking or burning. Any cracks in the cake will be concealed under the sour-cream glaze.

SOUR-CREAM GLAZE

- 2 cups sour cream
- ¼ cup sugar
- 1 teaspoon vanilla extract
- 1 teaspoon dark rum
- 2 tablespoons reserved streusel topping

Combine sour cream, sugar, vanilla, and rum with a rubber spatula in a plastic bowl. Spread evenly and smoothly over top of baked filling, sprinkle with streusel topping, and return to 350 degree F. oven for 10 minutes. Remove from oven and place **immediately** in refrigerator to cool. This prevents cracks from forming on top of the cake.

Before serving, let cheesecake stand at room temperature for 10 minutes to allow the butter in the crust to loosen its bond with the metal ring. When you release the springform clasp, the crust will generally detach naturally from the sides. If it sticks, separate crust from the sides gently with a metal spatula or a sharp knife.

Mocha Cheesecake

Preheat oven to 350 degrees F. If ingredients are not at room temperature, add five minutes to baking time.

CRUST

¼ pound (1 stick) lightly salted butter

2 cups finely ground chocolate-cookie crumbs

¼ cup sugar

Melt butter over very low heat. Combine butter with crumbs and sugar in a food processor until thoroughly blended or stir and mash together with a fork in a roomy bowl. Press small amounts of crust mix bit by bit all the way up the sides of an ungreased 10″ springform pan first, and then press over the bottom of the pan.

BATTER

4 ounces sweet chocolate

2 pounds (4 8-ounce packages) cream cheese

1¼ cups sugar

2 teaspoons instant espresso

1 tablespoon cognac

1½ teaspoons coffee-flavored liqueur

pinch of salt

4 large eggs

Melt sweet chocolate in the top of a double boiler, or in a microwave oven on half power, and reserve.

In a mixer, whip cream cheese on the highest speed for 5 minutes, then add sugar and whip for 2 minutes more. Dissolve espresso in cognac and coffee liqueurs. Add with salt and melted chocolate to the cream cheese and blend together thoroughly. Add the eggs, one at a time, keeping the mixer on the lowest speed in order to prevent too much air from destroying the proper consistency of the batter; mix just until each egg has been incorporated into the batter.

Pour batter into the crust and bake in a preheated oven for 50–55 minutes. Remove cake from oven and let stand on a countertop for 10 minutes while you prepare sour-cream glaze. This essential step allows the interior of the cake to solidify without overbaking or burning. Any cracks in the cake will be concealed under the sour-cream glaze.

SOUR-CREAM GLAZE

2 cups sour cream

¼ cup sugar

1 teaspoon coffee-flavored liqueur

Combine sour cream, sugar, and liqueur with a rubber spatula in a plastic bowl. Spread evenly and smoothly over top of baked filling and return to 350 degree F. oven for 10 minutes. Remove from oven and place **immediately** in refrigerator to cool. This prevents cracks from forming on top of the cake.

Before serving, let cheesecake stand at room temperature for 10 minutes to allow the butter in the crust to loosen its bond with the metal ring. When you release the springform clasp, the crust will generally detach naturally from the sides. If it sticks, separate crust from the sides gently with a metal spatula or a sharp knife.

Mocha Bianca Cheesecake

Preheat oven to 350 degrees F. If ingredients are not at room temperature, add five minutes to baking time.

CRUST

¼ pound (1 stick) lightly salted butter

2 cups very finely ground chocolate-cookie
   crumbs

¼ cup sugar

Melt butter over very low heat. Combine butter with crumbs and sugar in a food processor until thoroughly blended or stir and mash together with a fork in a roomy bowl. Press small amounts of crust mix bit by bit all the way up the sides of an ungreased 10″ springform pan first, and then press over the bottom of the pan.

BATTER

3 ounces white chocolate

2 pounds (4 8-ounce packages) cream cheese

1½ cups sugar

2 teaspoons instant espresso

1½ teaspoons coffee liqueur

1 tablespoon cognac

pinch of salt

4 large eggs

Melt white chocolate over simmering water in the top of a double boiler, or in a microwave oven on half power, and reserve.

In a mixer, whip cream cheese on the highest speed for 5 minutes, then add sugar and whip for 2 minutes more. Dissolve espresso in coffee liqueur and cognac, and add along with melted white chocolate and salt to the batter, and blend together thoroughly. Add the eggs, one at a time, keeping the mixer on the lowest speed in order to prevent too much air from destroying the proper consistency of the batter; mix just until each egg has been incorporated into the batter.

Pour batter into the crust and bake in a preheated oven for 50–55 minutes. Remove cake from oven and let stand on a countertop for 10 minutes while you prepare sour-cream glaze. This essential step allows the interior of the cake to solidify without overbaking or burning. Any cracks in the cake will be concealed under the sour-cream glaze.

SOUR-CREAM GLAZE

2 cups sour cream

¼ cup sugar

1 teaspoon coffee liqueur

1 ounce coffee-flavored chocolate bar, shaved
    or grated

Combine sour cream, sugar, and liqueur with a rubber spatula in a plastic bowl. Spread evenly and smoothly over top of baked filling and return to 350 degree F. oven for 10 minutes. Remove from oven, sprinkle grated chocolate on sour-cream glaze for garnish, and place **immediately** in refrigerator to cool to prevent cracks from forming in the cake.

Before serving, let cheesecake stand at room temperature for 10 minutes to allow the butter in the crust to loosen its bond with the metal ring. When you release the springform clasp, the crust will generally detach naturally from the sides. If it sticks, separate crust from the sides gently with a metal spatula or a sharp knife.

Irish Coffee Cheesecake

Preheat oven to 350 degrees F. If ingredients are not at room temperature, add five minutes to baking time.

CRUST

- ¼ pound (1 stick) lightly salted butter
- ½ cup coffee-flavored chocolate, grated
- 1½ cups finely ground chocolate-cookie crumbs
- ¼ cup sugar

Melt butter over very low heat. Combine butter, grated chocolate, crumbs and sugar in a food processor until thoroughly blended, or stir and mash together with a fork in a roomy bowl. Press small amounts of crust mix bit by bit all the way up the sides of ungreased 10″ springform pan first, and then press over the bottom of the pan.

BATTER

- 2 pounds (4 8-ounce packages) cream cheese
- 1¾ cups sugar
- 2 teaspoons instant espresso
- 1½ tablespoons Irish whiskey
- ½ teaspoon whiskey extract or flavoring
  pinch of salt
- 4 large eggs
- ¼ cup coffee-flavored chocolate, grated

In a mixer, whip cream cheese on the highest speed for 5 minutes, then add sugar and whip for 2 minutes more. Dissolve espresso in whiskey and whiskey extract or flavoring, add along with salt, and blend together thoroughly. Add the eggs, one at a time, keeping the mixer on the lowest speed in order to prevent too much air from destroying the proper consistency of the batter; mix just until each egg has been incorporated into the batter. Fold coffee-flavored chocolate into batter.

Pour batter into crust and bake in preheated oven for 55–60 minutes. Remove from oven and let stand on a countertop for 10 minutes while you prepare the sour-cream glaze. This essential step allows the interior of the cake to solidify without overbaking or burning. Any cracks in the cake will be concealed under the sour-cream glaze.

SOUR-CREAM GLAZE
2 cups sour cream

¼ cup sugar

1 teaspoon coffee liqueur

shaved coffee-flavored chocolate for garnish

Combine sour cream, sugar, and liqueur with a rubber spatula in a plastic bowl. Spread evenly and smoothly over top of baked filling and return to 350 degree F. oven for 10 minutes. Remove from oven, garnish with grated chocolate, and place in refrigerator immediately to cool. This prevents cracks from forming in the cake.

Before serving, let cheesecake stand at room temperature for 10 minutes to allow the butter in the crust to loosen its bond with the metal ring. When you release the springform clasp, the crust will generally detach naturally from the sides. If it sticks, separate crust from the sides gently with a metal spatula or a sharp knife.

Peanut Butter and Jelly Cheesecake

Preheat oven to 350 degrees F. If ingredients are not at room temperature, add five minutes to baking time.

CRUST

¼   pound (1 stick) lightly salted butter

1½   cups finely ground vanilla-wafer crumbs

½   cup chopped peanuts

¼   cup sugar

Melt butter over very low heat. Combine butter with crumbs, nuts, and sugar in a food processor until thoroughly blended or stir and mash together with a fork in a roomy bowl. Press small amounts of crust mix bit by bit all the way up the sides of an ungreased 10″ springform pan first, and then press over the bottom of the pan.

BATTER

2   pounds (4 8-ounce packages) cream cheese

1½   cups sugar

1   tablespoon dark rum

1½   teaspoons vanilla extract

pinch of salt

4   large eggs

⅓   cup raspberry preserves

¼   cup smooth peanut butter

In a mixer, whip cream cheese on the highest speed for 5 minutes, then add sugar and whip for 2 minutes more. Add rum, vanilla extract, and salt, and blend together thoroughly. Add the eggs, one at a time, keeping the mixer on the lowest speed in order to prevent too much air from destroying the proper consistency of the batter; mix just until each egg has been incorporated into the batter.

Remove one cup of batter and blend raspberry preserves into it thoroughly with a rubber spatula. Remove a second cup of batter and blend peanut butter into it thoroughly with a rubber spatula. Pour remaining batter into the crust. Pour peanut-flavored batter into the center of the filling. Pour raspberry-flavored batter in a circle around the rim. Cut through both with a knife to achieve a swirl effect.

Bake in a preheated oven for 50–55 minutes. Remove cake from oven and let stand on a countertop for 10 minutes while you prepare sour-cream glaze. This essential step allows the interior of the cake to solidify without overbaking or burning. Any cracks in the cake will be concealed under the sour-cream glaze.

SOUR-CREAM GLAZE

2 cups sour cream

¼ cup sugar

1 teaspoon dark rum

2 tablespoons chopped peanuts

Combine sour cream, sugar, and rum with a rubber spatula in a plastic bowl. Spread evenly and smoothly over top of baked filling, sprinkle with chopped peanuts, and return to 350 degree F. oven for 10 minutes. Remove from oven and place **immediately** in refrigerator to cool. This prevents cracks from forming on top of the cake.

Before serving, let cheesecake stand at room temperature for 10 minutes to allow the butter in the crust to loosen its bond with the metal ring. When you release the springform clasp, the crust will generally detach naturally from the sides. If it sticks, separate crust from the sides gently with a metal spatula or a sharp knife.

Raspberry Trifle Cheesecake

Preheat oven to 350 degrees F. If ingredients are not at room temperature, add five minutes to baking time.

CRUST

¼ pound (1 stick) lightly salted butter

2 cups finely ground ladyfinger crumbs

¼ cup sugar

Melt butter over very low heat. Combine butter with crumbs and sugar in a food processor until thoroughly blended or stir and mash together with a fork in a roomy bowl. Press small amounts of crust mix bit by bit all the way up the sides of an ungreased 10″ springform pan first, and then press over the bottom of the pan.

BATTER

2 pounds (4 8-ounce packages) cream cheese

1¼ cups sugar

1½ teaspoons almond extract

1 tablespoon triple sec

pinch of salt

4 large eggs

¼ cup blanched, sliced almonds, toasted

⅓ cup raspberry preserves

½ teaspoon raspberry extract

In a mixer, whip cream cheese on the highest speed for 5 minutes, then add sugar and whip for 2 minutes more. Add extract, triple sec, and salt and blend together thoroughly. Add the eggs, one at a time, keeping the mixer on the lowest speed in order to prevent too much air from destroying the proper consistency of the batter; mix just until each egg has been incorporated into the batter.

Remove one cup of batter and blend raspberry preserves and raspberry extract into it thoroughly with a rubber spatula. Blend the almonds into the remaining batter and pour it into the crust. Pour the raspberry batter into center of the cake and cut through with a knife to achieve a swirl effect. Bake in a preheated oven for 1 hour and 10 minutes. Remove cake from oven and let stand on a countertop for 10 minutes while you prepare sour-cream glaze. This essential step allows the interior of the cake to solidify without overbaking or burning. Any cracks in the cake will be concealed under the sour-cream glaze.

SOUR-CREAM GLAZE
2 cups sour cream

¼ cup sugar

1 teaspoon almond extract

¼ cup blanched, sliced almonds, toasted

Combine sour cream, sugar, and extract with a rubber spatula in a plastic bowl. Spread evenly and smoothly over top of baked filling, sprinkle with almonds, and return to 350 degree F. oven for 10 minutes. Remove from oven and place **immediately** in refrigerator to cool. This prevents cracks from forming on top of the cake.

Before serving, let cheesecake stand at room temperature for 10 minutes to allow the butter in the crust to loosen its bond with the metal ring. When you release the springform clasp, the crust will generally detach naturally from the sides. If it sticks, separate crust from the sides gently with a metal spatula or a sharp knife.

Chocolate Swirl Cheesecake

Preheat oven to 350 degrees F. If ingredients are not at room temperature, add five minutes to baking time.

CRUST

¼   pound (1 stick) lightly salted butter

2   cups finely ground chocolate-cookie crumbs

¼   cup sugar

Melt butter over very low heat. Combine butter with crumbs and sugar in a food processor until thoroughly blended or stir and mash together with a fork in a roomy bowl. Press small amounts of crust mix bit by bit all the way up the sides of an ungreased 10″ springform pan first, and then press over the bottom of the pan.

BATTER

2   ounces sweet chocolate

2   pounds (4 8-ounce packages) cream cheese

1½   cups sugar

1½   tablespoons dark rum

1½   teaspoons vanilla extract

    pinch of salt

4   large eggs

¼   teaspoon instant espresso

Melt chocolate in a double boiler over simmering water or in a microwave on half power, and reserve.

In a mixer, whip cream cheese on the highest speed for 5 minutes, then add sugar and whip for 2 minutes more. Add rum, vanilla, and salt, and blend together thoroughly. Add the eggs, one at a time, keeping the mixer on the lowest speed in order to prevent too much air from destroying the proper consistency of the batter; mix just until each egg has been incorporated into the batter.

Remove one cup of batter, add melted chocolate and instant espresso to it, blend thoroughly with a rubber spatula and reserve. Pour remaining batter into the crust. Pour reserved batter into the center of the filling and cut through several times with a knife to achieve a swirl effect, but with most of the chocolate batter remaining in the center. Bake in a preheated oven for one hour. Remove cake from oven and let stand on a countertop for 10 minutes while you prepare sour-cream glaze. This essential step allows the interior of the cake to solidify without overbaking or burning. Any cracks in the cake will be concealed under the sour-cream glaze.

SOUR-CREAM GLAZE

- 2 cups sour cream
- ¼ cup sugar
- 1 teaspoon almond extract
- 2 ounces sweet chocolate, melted

Combine sour cream, sugar, and extract with a rubber spatula in a plastic bowl. Spread evenly and smoothly over top of baked filling and return to 350 degree F. oven for 10 minutes. Remove from oven, dribble melted chocolate on the glaze in a Jackson Pollock pattern, and place **immediately** in refrigerator to cool. This prevents cracks from forming on top of the cake.

Before serving, let cheesecake stand at room temperature for 10 minutes to allow the butter in the crust to loosen its bond with the metal ring. When you release the springform clasp, the crust will generally detach naturally from the sides. If it sticks, separate crust from the sides gently with a metal spatula or a sharp knife.

Rum Raisin Cheesecake

Preheat oven to 350 degrees F. If ingredients are not at room temperature, add five minutes to baking time.

PRELIMINARY
½ cup golden raisins
½ cup dark raisins
1½ tablespoons dark rum

Soak raisins in rum for at least 15 minutes and reserve.

CRUST
¼ pound (1 stick) lightly salted butter
2 cups finely ground vanilla-wafer crumbs
¼ cup sugar

Melt butter over very low heat. Combine butter with crumbs and sugar in a food processor until thoroughly blended or stir and mash together with a fork in a roomy bowl. Press small amounts of crust mix bit by bit all the way up the sides of an ungreased 10″ springform pan first, and then press over the bottom of the pan.

BATTER
2 pounds (4 8-ounce packages) cream cheese
1½ cups sugar
1 teaspoon vanilla extract
reserved raisins and rum
½ teaspoon rum extract
pinch of salt
4 large eggs
1 egg yolk

In a mixer, whip cream cheese on the highest speed for 5 minutes, then add sugar and whip for 2 minutes more. Add extracts, reserved raisins and rum, and salt and blend together thoroughly. Add the eggs and the yolk, one at a time, keeping the mixer on the lowest speed in order to prevent too much air from destroying the proper consistency of the batter; mix just until each egg has been incorporated into the batter.

Pour batter into the crust and bake in a preheated oven for 50–55 minutes. Remove cake from oven and let stand on a countertop for 10 minutes while you prepare sour-cream glaze. This essential step allows the interior of the cake to solidify without overbaking or burning. Any cracks in the cake will be concealed under the sour-cream glaze.

SOUR-CREAM GLAZE

2 cups sour cream

¼ cup sugar

1 teaspoon dark rum

Combine sour cream, sugar, and rum with a rubber spatula in a plastic bowl. Spread evenly and smoothly over top of baked filling and return to 350 degree F. oven for 10 minutes. Remove from oven and place **immediately** in refrigerator to cool. This prevents cracks from forming on top of the cake.

Before serving, let cheesecake stand at room temperature for 10 minutes to allow the butter in the crust to loosen its bond with the metal ring. When you release the springform clasp, the crust will generally detach naturally from the sides. If it sticks, separate crust from the sides gently with a metal spatula or a sharp knife.

Jamoca Cheesecake

Preheat oven to 350 degrees F. If ingredients are not at room temperature, add five minutes to baking time.

CRUST
¼ pound (1 stick) lightly salted butter
2 cups finely ground chocolate-cookie crumbs
¼ cup sugar

Melt butter over very low heat. Combine butter with crumbs and sugar in a food processor until thoroughly blended or stir and mash together with a fork in a roomy bowl. Press small amounts of crust mix bit by bit all the way up the sides of an ungreased 10″ springform pan first, and then press over the bottom of the pan.

BATTER
2 ounces sweet chocolate
2 pounds (4 8-ounce packages) cream cheese
1½ cups sugar
1 teaspoon instant espresso
1½ tablespoons coffee-flavored liqueur
½ cup chopped walnuts
   pinch of salt
4 large eggs

Melt chocolate in a double boiler over simmering water or in a microwave on half power, and reserve.

In a mixer, whip cream cheese on the highest speed for 5 minutes, then add sugar and whip for 2 minutes more. Add espresso, liqueur, nuts, and salt and blend together thoroughly. Add the eggs, one at a time, keeping the mixer on the lowest speed in order to prevent too much air from destroying the proper consistency of the batter; mix just until each egg has been incorporated into the batter.

NOTE: If you use a food processor to prepare the batter, blend the ingredients well and add the eggs one at a time until they are just incorporated into the batter.

Remove one cup of batter, add melted chocolate to it, blend thoroughly with a rubber spatula, and reserve. Pour remaining batter into the crust. Pour reserved batter into the center of the filling and cut through several times with a knife to achieve a swirl effect, but with the most of the chocolate batter remaining in the center. Bake in a preheated oven for 1 hour and 10 minutes. Remove cake from oven and let stand on a countertop for 10 minutes while you prepare sour-cream glaze. This essential step allows the interior of the cake to solidify without overbaking or burning. Any cracks in the cake will be concealed under the sour-cream glaze.

SOUR-CREAM GLAZE

2 cups sour cream
¼ cup sugar
1 teaspoon coffee-flavored liqueur

Combine sour cream, sugar, and liqueur with a rubber spatula in a plastic bowl. Spread evenly and smoothly over top of baked filling and return to 350 degree F. oven for 10 minutes. Remove from oven and place **immediately** in refrigerator to cool. This prevents cracks from forming on top of the cake.

Before serving, let cheesecake stand at room temperature for 10 minutes to allow the butter in the crust to loosen its bond with the metal ring. When you release the springform clasp, the crust will generally detach naturally from the sides. If it sticks, separate crust from the sides gently with a metal spatula or a sharp knife.

Aniseed Cheesecake

Preheat oven to 350 degrees F. If ingredients are not at room temperature, add five minutes to baking time.

CRUST

¼ pound (1 stick) lightly salted butter
2 cups finely ground vanilla-wafer crumbs
¼ cup sugar

Melt butter over very low heat. Combine butter with crumbs and sugar in a food processor until thoroughly blended or stir and mash together with a fork in a roomy bowl. Press small amounts of crust mix bit by bit all the way up the sides of an ungreased 10″ springform pan first, and then press over the bottom of the pan.

BATTER

2 pounds (4 8-ounce packages) cream cheese
1½ cups sugar
1 tablespoon anisette
2 teaspoons anise extract
¼ cup poppyseed pastry filling
¼ cup pine nuts
   pinch of salt
4 large eggs

In a mixer, whip cream cheese on the highest speed for 5 minutes, then add sugar and whip for 2 minutes more. Add anisette, anise extract, poppyseed filling, pine nuts, and salt and blend together thoroughly. Add the eggs, one at a time, keeping the mixer on the lowest speed in order to prevent too much air from destroying the proper consistency of the batter; mix just until each egg has been incorporated into the batter.

Pour batter into the crust and bake in a preheated oven for 50–55 minutes. Remove cake from oven and let stand on a countertop for 10 minutes while you prepare sour-cream glaze. This essential step allows the interior of the

cake to solidify without overbaking or burning. Any cracks in the cake will be concealed under the sour-cream glaze.

SOUR-CREAM GLAZE

2 cups sour cream

¼ cup sugar

1 teaspoon anisette

Combine sour cream, sugar, and anisette with a rubber spatula in a plastic bowl. Spread evenly and smoothly over top of baked filling and return to 350 degree F. oven for 10 minutes. Remove from oven and place **immediately** in refrigerator to cool. This prevents cracks from forming on top of the cake.

Before serving, let cheesecake stand at room temperature for 10 minutes to allow the butter in the crust to loosen its bond with the metal ring. When you release the springform clasp, the crust will generally detach naturally from the sides. If it sticks, separate crust from the sides gently with a metal spatula or a sharp knife.

Cranberry Mint Cheesecake

Preheat oven to 350 degrees F. If ingredients are not at room temperature, add 5 minutes to baking time.

CRUST

¼ pound (1 stick) lightly salted butter
2 cups finely ground vanilla-wafer crumbs
¼ cup sugar

Melt butter over very low heat. Combine butter with crumbs and sugar in a food processor until thoroughly blended or stir and mash together with a fork in a roomy bowl. Press small amounts of crust mix bit by bit all the way up the sides of an ungreased 10″ springform pan first, and then press over the bottom of the pan.

BATTER

2 pounds (4 8-ounce packages) cream cheese
1½ cups sugar
1½ tablespoons mint extract
    pinch of salt
4 large eggs
2 cups fresh or frozen cranberries

In a mixer, whip cream cheese on the highest speed for 5 minutes, then add sugar and whip for 2 minutes more. Add extract and salt and blend together thoroughly. Add the eggs, one at a time, keeping the mixer on the lowest speed in order to prevent too much air from destroying the proper consistency of the batter; mix just until each egg has been incorporated into the batter. Fold in cranberries with a rubber spatula.

Pour batter into the crust and bake in a preheated oven for 50–55 minutes. Remove cake from oven and let stand on a countertop for 10 minutes while you prepare sour-cream glaze. This essential step allows the interior of the cake to solidify without overbaking or burning. Any cracks in the cake will be concealed under the sour-cream glaze.

SOUR-CREAM GLAZE

2 cups sour cream

¼ cup sugar

1 teaspoon white crème de menthe

Combine sour cream, sugar, and crème de menthe with a rubber spatula in a plastic bowl. Spread evenly and smoothly over top of baked filling and return to 350 degree F. oven for 10 minutes. Remove from oven and place **immediately** in refrigerator to cool. This prevents cracks from forming on top of the cake.

Before serving, let cheesecake stand at room temperature for 10 minutes to allow the butter in the crust to loosen its bond with the metal ring. When you release the springform clasp, the crust will generally detach naturally from the sides. If it sticks, separate crust from the sides gently with a metal spatula or a sharp knife.

White Cassis Cheesecake

Preheat oven to 350 degrees F. If ingredients are not at room temperature, add five minutes to baking time.

CRUST

¼ pound (1 stick) lightly salted butter

2 cups finely ground arrowroot-biscuit crumbs

1 ounce white chocolate, grated

¼ cup sugar

Melt butter over very low heat. Combine butter with crumbs, white chocolate, and sugar in a food processor until thoroughly blended or stir and mash together with a fork in a roomy bowl. Press small amounts of crust mix bit by bit all the way up the sides of an ungreased 10″ springform pan first, and then press over the bottom of the pan.

BATTER

2 pounds (4 8-ounce packages) cream cheese

1½ cups sugar

3 tablespoons cassis

pinch of salt

4 large eggs

3 ounces white chocolate, shaved or sliced very
thin

In a mixer, whip cream cheese on the highest speed for 5 minutes, then add sugar and whip for 2 minutes more. Add cassis and salt and blend together thoroughly. Add the eggs, one at a time, keeping the mixer on the lowest speed in order to prevent too much air from destroying the proper consistency of the batter; mix just until each egg has been incorporated into the batter. Fold in white chocolate.

Pour batter into the crust and bake in a preheated oven for 50–55 minutes. Remove cake from oven and let stand on a countertop for 10 minutes while you prepare sour-cream glaze. This essential step allows the interior of the

cake to solidify without overbaking or burning. Any cracks in the cake will be concealed under the sour-cream glaze.

SOUR-CREAM GLAZE

2 cups sour cream

¼ cup sugar

1 teaspoon almond extract

1 ounce white chocolate, shaved or sliced very thin

Combine sour cream, sugar, and extract with a rubber spatula in a plastic bowl. Spread evenly and smoothly over top of baked filling and return to 350 degree F. oven for 10 minutes. Remove from oven, garnish cake with shaved white chocolate, and place **immediately** in refrigerator to cool. This prevents cracks from forming on top of the cake.

Before serving, let cheesecake stand at room temperature for 10 minutes to allow the butter in the crust to loosen its bond with the metal ring. When you release the springform clasp, the crust will generally detach naturally from the sides. If it sticks, separate crust from the sides gently with a metal spatula or a sharp knife.

Hazelnut Cheesecake

Preheat oven to 350 degrees F. If ingredients are not at room temperature, add five minutes to baking time.

CRUST

¼ pound (1 stick) lightly salted butter

1½ cups finely ground vanilla-wafer crumbs

½ cup ground hazelnuts, toasted in a 350
     degree F. oven for no more than 10 minutes,
     and watched carefully to make sure they
     don't burn

¼ cup sugar

Melt butter over very low heat. Combine butter with crumbs, nuts, and sugar in a food processor until thoroughly blended or stir and mash together with a fork in a roomy bowl. Press small amounts of crust mix bit by bit all the way up the sides of an ungreased 10″ springform pan first, and then press over the bottom of the pan.

BATTER

2 pounds (4 8-ounce packages) cream cheese

1½ cups sugar

2 tablespoons Frangelico or praline liqueur

½ cup ground hazelnuts, toasted as above
     pinch of salt

4 large eggs

In a mixer, whip cream cheese on the highest speed for 5 minutes, then add sugar and whip for 2 minutes more. Add liqueur, nuts, and salt and blend together thoroughly. Add the eggs, one at a time, keeping the mixer on the lowest speed in order to prevent too much air from destroying the proper consistency of the batter; mix just until each egg has been incorporated into the batter.

Pour batter into the crust and bake in a preheated oven for 55–60 minutes.

Remove cake from oven and let stand on a countertop for 10 minutes while you prepare sour-cream glaze. This essential step allows the interior of the cake to solidify without overbaking or burning. Any cracks in the cake will be concealed under the sour-cream glaze.

SOUR-CREAM GLAZE

- 2 cups sour cream
- ¼ cup sugar
- 1 teaspoon Frangelico or praline liqueur
- 2 tablespoons ground hazelnuts, toasted as above

Combine sour cream, sugar, and liqueur with a rubber spatula in a plastic bowl. Spread evenly and smoothly over top of baked filling, sprinkle with hazelnuts, and return to 350 degree F. oven for 10 minutes. Remove from oven and place **immediately** in refrigerator to cool. This prevents cracks from forming on top of the cake.

Before serving, let cheesecake stand at room temperature for 10 minutes to allow the butter in the crust to loosen its bond with the metal ring. When you release the springform clasp, the crust will generally detach naturally from the sides. If it sticks, separate crust from the sides gently with a metal spatula or a sharp knife.

Chocolate-Almond Coconut Cheesecake

Preheat oven to 350 degrees F. If ingredients are not at room temperature, add five minutes to baking time.

CRUST

¼ pound (1 stick) lightly salted butter
2 cups finely ground chocolate-cookie crumbs
¼ cup sugar

Melt butter over very low heat. Combine butter with crumbs and sugar in a food processor until thoroughly blended or stir and mash together with a fork in a roomy bowl. Press small amounts of crust mix bit by bit all the way up the sides of an ungreased 10″ springform pan first, and then press over the bottom of the pan.

BATTER

2 pounds (4 8-ounce packages) cream cheese
1½ cups sugar
1 teaspoon amaretto
1 teaspoon almond extract
½ cup coarsely chopped almonds
   pinch of salt
4 large eggs

In a mixer, whip cream cheese on the highest speed for 5 minutes, then add sugar and whip for 2 minutes more. Add amaretto, extract, almonds, and salt and blend together thoroughly. Add the eggs, one at a time, keeping the mixer on the lowest speed in order to prevent too much air from destroying the proper consistency of the batter; mix just until each egg has been incorporated into the batter.

Pour batter into the crust and bake in a preheated oven for 50–55 minutes. Remove cake from oven and let stand on a countertop for 10 minutes while you prepare sour-cream glaze. This essential step allows the interior of the

cake to solidify without overbaking or burning. Any cracks in the cake will be concealed under the sour-cream glaze.

SOUR-CREAM GLAZE
- 2 cups sour cream
- ¼ cup sugar
- 1 teaspoon coconut extract
- ¼ cup blanched, sliced almonds, toasted
- ½ cup coconut flakes

Combine sour cream, sugar, and extract with a rubber spatula in a plastic bowl. Spread evenly and smoothly over top of baked filling, sprinkle with nuts and coconut, and return to 350 degree F. oven for 10 minutes. Remove from oven and place **immediately** in refrigerator to cool. This prevents cracks from forming on top of the cake.

Before serving, let cheesecake stand at room temperature for 10 minutes to allow the butter in the crust to loosen its bond with the metal ring. When you release the springform clasp, the crust will generally detach naturally from the sides. If it sticks, separate crust from the sides gently with a metal spatula or a sharp knife.

Four-Chocolate Cheesecake

Preheat oven to 350 degrees F. If ingredients are not at room temperature, add 5 minutes to baking time.

CRUST

¼ pound (1 stick) lightly salted butter
1 cup finely ground vanilla-wafer crumbs
1 cup finely ground chocolate-wafer crumbs
¼ cup sugar

Melt butter over very low heat. Combine butter with crumbs and sugar in a food processor until thoroughly blended or stir and mash together with a fork in a roomy bowl. Press small amounts of crust mix bit by bit all the way up the sides of an ungreased 10″ springform pan first, and then press over the bottom of the pan.

BATTER

1 ounce sweet chocolate
3 ounces white chocolate
2 pounds (4 8-ounce packages) cream cheese
1¼ cups sugar
1 tablespoon Grand Marnier
1½ teaspoons orange extract
pinch of salt
4 large eggs
1 orange-flavored chocolate bar, grated or
chopped

Melt the sweet and the white chocolate separately in a double boiler over simmering water or in a microwave on half power, and reserve.

In a mixer, whip cream cheese on the highest speed for 5 minutes, then add sugar and whip for 2 minutes more. Add Grand Marnier, orange extract, and salt and blend together thoroughly. Add the eggs, one at a time, keeping the mixer on the lowest speed in order to prevent too much air from destroying the proper consistency of the batter; mix just until each egg has been incorporated into the batter.

Add melted sweet chocolate to one cup of batter with a rubber spatula and set aside. Add melted white chocolate and the grated orange-flavored chocolate to the remaining batter and pour into crust. Pour reserved chocolate batter into the center of the pan and cut through several times with a knife to achieve a swirl effect. Bake in a preheated oven for 50–55 minutes. Remove cake from oven and let stand on a countertop for 10 minutes while you prepare sour-cream glaze. This essential step allows the interior of the cake to solidify without overbaking or burning. Any cracks in the cake will be concealed under the sour-cream glaze.

SOUR-CREAM GLAZE

2 cups sour cream

¼ cup sugar

1 teaspoon Grand Marnier

1 ounce orange-flavored chocolate, melted

Combine sour cream, sugar, and Grand Marnier with a rubber spatula in a plastic bowl. Spread evenly and smoothly over top of baked filling and return to 350 degree F. oven for 10 minutes. Remove from oven, dribble melted orange-flavored chocolate on the crust, and place **immediately** in refrigerator to cool. This prevents cracks from forming on top of the cake.

Before serving, let cheesecake stand at room temperature for 10 minutes to allow the butter in the crust to loosen its bond with the metal ring. When you release the springform clasp, the crust will generally detach naturally from the sides. If it sticks, separate crust from the sides gently with a metal spatula or a sharp knife.

Southern Peach Cheesecake

Preheat oven to 350 degrees F. If ingredients are not at room temperature, add five minutes to baking time.

CRUST

¼   pound (1 stick) lightly salted butter
1½ cups finely ground nut-cookie crumbs
½   cup finely chopped pecans
¼   cup sugar

Melt butter over very low heat. Combine butter with crumbs, nuts, and sugar in a food processor until thoroughly blended or stir and mash together with a fork in a roomy bowl. Press small amounts of crust mix bit by bit all the way up the sides of an ungreased 10″ springform pan first, and then press over the bottom of the pan.

BATTER

2   pounds (4 8-ounce packages) cream cheese
1   cup sugar
1   tablespoon peach extract
1½ teaspoons vanilla extract
    pinch of salt
4   large eggs
½   cup peach preserves
½   cup coconut flakes
½   cup chopped pecans

In a mixer, whip cream cheese on the highest speed for 5 minutes, then add sugar and whip for 2 minutes more. Add extracts and salt and blend together thoroughly. Add the eggs, one at a time, keeping the mixer on the lowest speed in order to prevent too much air from destroying the proper consistency of the batter; mix just until each egg has been incorporated into the batter.

Remove one cup of batter and stir peach preserves and coconut flakes into it. Add nuts to the batter remaining in the mixer and pour half of this batter into the crust. Spread a layer of peach-and-coconut-flavored batter, over it and then cover with the remaining nut-flavored batter. Bake in a preheated oven for 50–55 minutes. Remove cake from oven and let stand on a countertop for 10 minutes while you prepare sour-cream glaze. This essential step allows the interior of the cake to solidify without overbaking or burning. Any cracks in the cake will be concealed under the sour-cream glaze.

SOUR-CREAM GLAZE

- 2 cups sour cream
- ¼ cup sugar
- 1 teaspoon almond extract
- 2 tablespoons chopped pecans

Combine sour cream, sugar, and extract with a rubber spatula in a plastic bowl. Spread evenly and smoothly over top of baked filling, sprinkle nuts on top, and return to 350 degree F. oven for 10 minutes. Remove from oven and place **immediately** in refrigerator to cool. This prevents cracks from forming on top of the cake.

Before serving, let cheesecake stand at room temperature for 10 minutes to allow the butter in the crust to loosen its bond with the metal ring. When you release the springform clasp, the crust will generally detach naturally from the sides. If it sticks, separate crust from the sides gently with a metal spatula or a sharp knife.

Munich Cheesecake

Preheat oven to 350 degrees F. If ingredients are not at room temperature, add five minutes to baking time.

This cheesecake has no crust, which is why the springform pan must be greased.

BATTER

3 pounds (6 8-ounce packages) cream cheese
2 cups sugar
1 tablespoon lime juice
1 tablespoon orange extract
  pinch of salt
6 large eggs

In a mixer, whip cream cheese on the highest speed for 5 minutes, then add sugar and whip for 2 minutes more. Add lime juice, extract, and salt and blend together thoroughly. Add the eggs, one at a time, keeping the mixer on the lowest speed in order to prevent too much air from destroying the proper consistency of the batter; mix just until each egg has been incorporated into the batter.

Pour batter into greased springform pan and bake in a preheated oven for 1 hour and 5–10 minutes. Remove cake from oven and let stand on a countertop for 10 minutes while you prepare sour-cream glaze. This essential step allows the interior of the cake to solidify without overbaking or burning.

TOPPING

1 cup chopped walnuts
¼ cup flour
¼ cup softened butter
½ teaspoon cinnamon
½ cup brown sugar
½ cup white raisins

Combine walnuts, flour, butter, cinnamon, and sugar in a food processor until well blended. Mix raisins in with a spoon. Coat baked cheesecake with the topping and return to 350 degree F. oven for 10 minutes. Remove from oven and place **immediately** in refrigerator to cool. This prevents cracks from forming on top of the cake.

Right before serving, turn the cheesecake upside down to remove it from the springform pan, so the topping is on the bottom of the cake.

Zabaglione Cheesecake

Preheat oven to 350 degrees F. If ingredients are not at room temperature, add five minutes to baking time.

CRUST

¼ pound (1 stick) lightly salted butter

2 cups finely ground Italian wine-biscuit crumbs

¼ cup sugar

Melt butter over very low heat. Combine butter with crumbs and sugar in a food processor until thoroughly blended or stir and mash together with a fork in a roomy bowl. Press small amounts of crust mix bit by bit all the way up the sides of an ungreased 10″ springform pan first, and then press over the bottom of the pan.

BATTER

2 pounds (4 8-ounce packages) cream cheese

1½ cups sugar

1 tablespoon eggnog flavoring

½ teaspoon brandy extract

1 teaspoon sweet Marsala

pinch of salt

4 large eggs

1 egg yolk

In a mixer whip cream cheese on the highest speed for 5 minutes, then add sugar and whip for 2 minutes more. Add flavoring, extract, Marsala, and salt, and blend together thoroughly. Add the eggs and the yolk, one at a time, keeping the mixer on the lowest speed in order to prevent too much air from destroying the proper consistency of the batter; mix just until each egg has been incorporated into the batter.

Pour batter into the crust and bake in a preheated oven for 50–55 minutes. Remove cake from oven and let stand on a countertop for 10 minutes while you prepare sour-cream glaze. This essential step allows the interior of the

cake to solidify without overbaking or burning. Any cracks in the cake will be concealed under the sour-cream glaze.

SOUR-CREAM GLAZE

2 cups sour cream

¼ cup sugar

1 teaspoon eggnog flavoring

Combine sour cream, sugar, and eggnog flavoring with a rubber spatula in a plastic bowl. Spread evenly and smoothly over top of baked filling and return to 350 degree F. oven for 10 minutes. Remove from oven and place **immediately** in refrigerator to cool. This prevents cracks from forming on top of the cake.

Before serving, let cheesecake stand at room temperature for 10 minutes to allow the butter in the crust to loosen its bond with the metal ring. When you release the springform clasp, the crust will generally detach naturally from the sides. If it sticks, separate crust from the sides gently with a metal spatula or a sharp knife.

Amaretto Cheesecake

Preheat oven to 350 degrees F. If ingredients are not at room temperature, add five minutes to baking time.

CRUST

¼ pound (1 stick) lightly salted butter

2 cups finely ground almond-flavored biscotti
   crumbs

¼ cup sugar

Melt butter over very low heat. Combine butter with crumbs and sugar in a food processor until thoroughly blended or stir and mash together with a fork in a roomy bowl. Press small amounts of crust mix bit by bit all the way up the sides of an ungreased 10″ springform pan first, and then press over the bottom of the pan.

BATTER

2 pounds (4 8-ounce packages) cream cheese

1½ cups sugar

1 tablespoon amaretto liqueur

1 teaspoon vanilla extract

1 teaspoon almond extract
   pinch of salt

4 large eggs

In a mixer, whip cream cheese on the highest speed for 5 minutes, then add sugar and whip for 2 minutes more. Add liqueur, extracts, and salt and blend together thoroughly. Add the eggs, one at a time, keeping the mixer on the lowest speed in order to prevent too much air from destroying the proper consistency of the batter; mix just until each egg has been incorporated into the batter.

Pour batter into the crust and bake in a preheated oven for 50–55 minutes. Remove cake from oven and let stand on a countertop for 10 minutes while you prepare sour-cream glaze. This essential step allows the interior of the

cake to solidify without overbaking or burning. Any cracks in the cake will be concealed under the sour-cream glaze.

SOUR-CREAM GLAZE

2 cups sour cream

¼ cup sugar

1 teaspoon almond extract or amaretto liqueur

½ cup blanched, sliced almonds, toasted

Combine sour cream, sugar, and extract or liqueur with a rubber spatula in a plastic bowl. Spread evenly and smoothly over top of baked filling, sprinkle with almonds, and return to 350 degree F. oven for 10 minutes. Remove from oven and place **immediately** in refrigerator to cool. This prevents cracks from forming on top of the cake.

Before serving, let cheesecake stand at room temperature for 10 minutes to allow the butter in the crust to loosen its bond with the metal ring. When you release the springform clasp, the crust will generally detach naturally from the sides. If it sticks, separate crust from the sides gently with a metal spatula or a sharp knife.

Praline Cheesecake

Preheat oven to 350 degrees F. If ingredients are not at room temperature, add five minutes to baking time.

CRUST

¼ pound (1 stick) lightly salted butter

1 cup finely ground vanilla-wafer crumbs

1 cup finely chopped pecans

2 tablespoons white sugar

2 tablespoons brown sugar

Melt butter over very low heat. Combine butter with crumbs, nuts, and sugars in a food processor until thoroughly blended or stir and mash together with a fork in a roomy bowl. Press small amounts of crust mix bit by bit all the way up the sides of an ungreased 10″ springform pan first, and then press over the bottom of the pan.

BATTER

2 pounds (4 8-ounce packages) cream cheese

¾ cup white sugar

¾ cup brown sugar, firmly packed

3 tablespoons praline liqueur or dark rum

½ cup pecan or cashew brittle, chopped

    pinch of salt

4 large eggs

In a mixer, whip cream cheese on the highest speed for 5 minutes, then add sugars and whip for 2 minutes more. Add liqueur or rum, brittle, and salt and blend together thoroughly. Add the eggs, one at a time, keeping the mixer on the lowest speed in order to prevent too much air from destroying the proper consistency of the batter; mix just until each egg has been incorporated into the batter.

Pour batter into the crust and bake in a preheated oven for 50–55 minutes. Remove cake from oven and let stand on a countertop for 10 minutes while

you prepare sour-cream glaze. This essential step allows the interior of the cake to solidify without overbaking or burning. Any cracks in the cake will be concealed under the sour-cream glaze.

SOUR-CREAM GLAZE

- 2 cups sour cream
- ¼ cup brown sugar, firmly packed
- 1 teaspoon praline liqueur or dark rum
- ½ teaspoon maple syrup
- ½ cup pecan or cashew brittle, chopped

Combine sour cream, sugar, and liqueur or rum and maple syrup with a rubber spatula in a plastic bowl. Spread evenly and smoothly over top of baked filling, sprinkle with brittle, and return to 350 degree F. oven for 10 minutes. Remove from oven and place **immediately** in refrigerator to cool. This prevents cracks from forming on top of the cake.

Before serving, let cheesecake stand at room temperature for 10 minutes to allow the butter in the crust to loosen its bond with the metal ring. When you release the springform clasp, the crust will generally detach naturally from the sides. If it sticks, separate crust from the sides gently with a metal spatula or a sharp knife.

Southern Coffee Cheesecake

Preheat oven to 350 degrees F. If ingredients are not at room temperature, add five minutes to baking time.

CRUST

¼ pound (1 stick) lightly salted butter

2 cups finely ground vanilla-wafer crumbs

¼ cup sugar

Melt butter over very low heat. Combine butter with crumbs and sugar in a food processor until thoroughly blended or stir and mash together with a fork in a roomy bowl. Press small amounts of crust mix bit by bit all the way up the sides of an ungreased 10″ springform pan first, and then press over the bottom of the pan.

BATTER

2 ounces white chocolate

2 pounds (4 8-ounce packages) cream cheese

1½ cups sugar

1 teaspoon instant espresso

½ cup pecans, chopped

1 tablespoon coffee-flavored liqueur

pinch of salt

4 large eggs

Melt white chocolate in a double boiler over simmering water, or in a microwave on half power, and reserve.

In a mixer, whip cream cheese on the highest speed for 5 minutes, then add sugar and whip for 2 minutes more. Add espresso, pecans, liqueur, and salt and blend together thoroughly. Add the eggs, one at a time, keeping the mixer on the lowest speed in order to prevent too much air from destroying the proper consistency of the batter; mix just until each egg has been incorporated into the batter.

Remove one cup of batter, blend melted white chocolate into it with a rubber spatula, and reserve. Pour half of the remaining batter into the crust, spread white chocolate batter over it, cover with the remaining batter in the mixer bowl, and bake in a preheated oven for 55–60 minutes. Remove cake from oven and let stand on a countertop for 10 minutes while you prepare sour-cream glaze. This essential step allows the interior of the cake to solidify without overbaking or burning. Any cracks in the cake will be concealed under the sour-cream glaze.

SOUR-CREAM GLAZE

- 2 cups sour cream
- ¼ cup sugar
- 1 teaspoon coffee-flavored liqueur

Combine sour cream, sugar, and liqueur with a rubber spatula in a plastic bowl. Spread evenly and smoothly over top of baked filling and return to 350 degree F. oven for 10 minutes. Remove from oven and place **immediately** in refrigerator to cool. This prevents cracks from forming on top of the cake.

Before serving, let cheesecake stand at room temperature for 10 minutes to allow the butter in the crust to loosen its bond with the metal ring. When you release the springform clasp, the crust will generally detach naturally from the sides. If it sticks, separate crust from the sides gently with a metal spatula or a sharp knife.

Chestnut Cheesecake

Preheat oven to 350 degrees F. If ingredients are not at room temperature, add five minutes to baking time.

CRUST
- ¼ pound (1 stick) lightly salted butter
- 2 cups finely ground gingersnap-cookie crumbs
- ¼ cup sugar

Melt butter over very low heat. Combine butter with crumbs and sugar in a food processor until thoroughly blended or stir and mash together with a fork in a roomy bowl. Press small amounts of crust mix bit by bit all the way up the sides of an ungreased 10″ springform pan first, and then press over the bottom of the pan.

BATTER
- 2 pounds (4 8-ounce packages) cream cheese
- 1½ cups sugar
- ½ cup sweetened chestnut puree
- 1½ tablespoons Drambuie
- 1 ounce crystallized ginger, cut into slivers
- pinch of salt
- 4 large eggs

In a mixer, whip cream cheese on the highest speed for 5 minutes, then add sugar and whip for 2 minutes more. Add chestnut puree, Drambuie, crystallized ginger, and salt and blend together thoroughly. Add the eggs, one at a time, keeping the mixer on the lowest speed in order to prevent too much air from destroying the proper consistency of the batter; mix just until each egg has been incorporated into the batter.

Pour batter into the crust and bake in a preheated oven for 55–60 minutes. Remove cake from oven and let stand on a countertop for 10 minutes while you prepare sour-cream glaze. This essential step allows the interior of the

cake to solidify without overbaking or burning. Any cracks in the cake will be concealed under the sour-cream glaze.

SOUR-CREAM GLAZE
2 cups sour cream
¼ cup sugar
1 teaspoon Drambuie
5 drops ginger extract

Combine sour cream, sugar, Drambuie, and extract with a rubber spatula in a plastic bowl. Spread evenly and smoothly over top of baked filling and return to 350 degree F. oven for 10 minutes. Remove from oven and place **immediately** in refrigerator to cool. This prevents cracks from forming on top of the cake.

Before serving, let cheesecake stand at room temperature for 10 minutes to allow the butter in the crust to loosen its bond with the metal ring. When you release the springform clasp, the crust will generally detach naturally from the sides. If it sticks, separate crust from the sides gently with a metal spatula or a sharp knife.

Mincemeat Cheesecake

Preheat oven to 350 degrees F. If ingredients are not at room temperature, add five minutes to baking time.

CRUST
¼ pound (1 stick) lightly salted butter
2 cups finely ground gingersnap-cookie crumbs
¼ cup sugar

Melt butter over very low heat. Combine butter with crumbs and sugar in a food processor until thoroughly blended or stir and mash together with a fork in a roomy bowl. Press small amounts of crust mix bit by bit all the way up the sides of an ungreased 10″ springform pan first, and then press over the bottom of the pan.

BATTER
2 pounds (4 8-ounce packages) cream cheese
1½ cups sugar
1½ tablespoons cognac
½ cup mincemeat
pinch of salt
4 large eggs

In a mixer, whip cream cheese on the highest speed for 5 minutes, then add sugar and whip for 2 minutes more. Add cognac, mincemeat, and salt and blend together thoroughly. Add the eggs, one at a time, keeping the mixer on the lowest speed in order to prevent too much air from destroying the proper consistency of the batter; mix just until each egg has been incorporated into the batter.

Pour batter into the crust and bake in a preheated oven for 50–55 minutes. Remove cake from oven and let stand on a countertop for 10 minutes while you prepare sour-cream glaze. This essential step allows the interior of the cake to solidify without overbaking or burning. Any cracks in the cake will be concealed under the sour-cream glaze.

SOUR-CREAM GLAZE

2 cups sour cream

¼ cup sugar

1 teaspoon cognac

Combine sour cream, sugar, and cognac with a rubber spatula in a plastic bowl. Spread evenly and smoothly over top of baked filling and return to 350 degree F. oven for 10 minutes. Remove from oven and place **immediately** in refrigerator to cool. This prevents cracks from forming on top of the cake.

Before serving, let cheesecake stand at room temperature for 10 minutes to allow the butter in the crust to loosen its bond with the metal ring. When you release the springform clasp, the crust will generally detach naturally from the sides. If it sticks, separate crust from the sides gently with a metal spatula or a sharp knife.

Nut Sundae Cheesecake

Preheat oven to 350 degrees F. If ingredients are not at room temperature, add five minutes to baking time.

CRUST

¼   pound (1 stick) lightly salted butter
½   cup finely ground vanilla-wafer crumbs
½   cup finely ground chocolate-wafer crumbs
½   cup walnut pieces
¼   cup sugar

Melt butter over very low heat. Combine butter with crumbs, nuts, and sugar in a food processor until thoroughly blended or stir and mash together with a fork in a roomy bowl. Press small amounts of crust mix bit by bit all the way up the sides of an ungreased 10″ springform pan first, and then press over the bottom of the pan.

BATTER

2   pounds (4 8-ounce packages) cream cheese
1¼   cups sugar
⅓   cup "wet" nuts, like those used in sundaes
1   cup nut butter mixed with chocolate, like
      Nutella
1½   tablespoons rum
1   teaspoon vanilla extract
      pinch of salt
4   large eggs
¼   cup chocolate fudge topping

In a mixer, whip cream cheese on the highest speed for 5 minutes, then add sugar and whip for 2 minutes more. Add nuts, nut butter, rum, vanilla, and salt and blend together thoroughly. Add the eggs, one at a time, keeping the mixer on the lowest speed in order to prevent too much air from destroying the proper consistency of the batter; mix just until each egg has been incorporated into the batter.

Pour batter into the crust. Warm bottle of fudge topping in hot water and dribble topping over the top of the batter. Cut into the batter with a knife to achieve a swirl effect, and bake in a preheated oven for 55–60 minutes. Remove cake from oven and let stand on a countertop for 10 minutes while you prepare sour-cream glaze. This essential step allows the interior of the cake to solidify without overbaking or burning. Any cracks in the cake will be concealed under the sour-cream glaze.

SOUR-CREAM GLAZE

2 cups sour cream

¼ cup sugar

1 teaspoon vanilla extract

chocolate fudge topping

Combine sour cream, sugar, and vanilla with a rubber spatula in a plastic bowl. Spread evenly and smoothly over top of baked filling, dribble fudge topping on glaze, and make a decorative swirl with the point of a knife. Return to 350 degree F. oven for 10 minutes. Remove from oven and place **immediately** in refrigerator to cool. This prevents cracks from forming on top of the cake.

Before serving, let cheesecake stand at room temperature for 10 minutes to allow the butter in the crust to loosen its bond with the metal ring. When you release the springform clasp, the crust will generally detach naturally from the sides. If it sticks, separate crust from the sides gently with a metal spatula or a sharp knife.

Middle Eastern Halvah Cheesecake

Preheat oven to 350 degrees F. If ingredients are not at room temperature, add five minutes to baking time.

CRUST

¼ pound (1 stick) lightly salted butter

1 cup finely ground vanilla-wafer crumbs

1 cup finely chopped walnuts

¼ cup sugar

Melt butter over very low heat. Combine butter with crumbs, nuts, and sugar in a food processor until thoroughly blended or stir and mash together with a fork in a roomy bowl. Press small amounts of crust mix bit by bit all the way up the sides of an ungreased 10″ springform pan first, and then press over the bottom of the pan.

BATTER

2 pounds (4 8-ounce packages) cream cheese

1⅓ cups sugar

1 tablespoon cream sherry

1 teaspoon sherry extract

pinch of salt

4 large eggs

6 ounces marble halvah, cut or chopped into
¼ inch bits

In a mixer, whip cream cheese on the highest speed for 5 minutes, then add sugar and whip for 2 minutes more. Add sherry, sherry extract, and salt and blend together thoroughly. Add the eggs, one at a time, keeping the mixer on the lowest speed in order to prevent too much air from destroying the proper consistency of the batter; mix just until each egg has been incorporated into the batter. Fold halvah into batter with a rubber spatula.

Pour batter into the crust and bake in a preheated oven for 50–55 minutes. Remove cake from oven and let stand on a countertop for 10 minutes while

you prepare sour-cream glaze. This essential step allows the interior of the cake to solidify without overbaking or burning. Any cracks in the cake will be concealed under the sour-cream glaze.

SOUR-CREAM GLAZE

2 cups sour cream

¼ cup sugar

1 teaspoon cream sherry

2 ounces halvah, chopped coarsely

Combine sour cream, sugar, and sherry with a rubber spatula in a plastic bowl. Spread evenly and smoothly over top of baked filling and return to 350 degree F. oven for 10 minutes. Remove from oven and place **immediately** in refrigerator to cool. This prevents cracks from forming on top of the cake.

Before serving, sprinkle with halvah and let cheesecake stand at room temperature for 10 minutes to allow the butter in the crust to loosen its bond with the metal ring. When you release the springform clasp, the crust will generally detach naturally from the sides. If it sticks, separate crust from the sides gently with a metal spatula or a sharp knife.

Chocolate Raspberry Cheesecake

Preheat oven to 350 degrees F. If ingredients are not at room temperature, add five minutes to baking time.

CRUST

¼ pound (1 stick) lightly salted butter

2 cups finely ground chocolate-wafer or cookie crumbs

¼ cup sugar

Melt butter over very low heat. Combine butter with crumbs and sugar in a food processor until thoroughly blended or stir and mash together with a fork in a roomy bowl. Press small amounts of crust mix bit by bit all the way up the sides of an ungreased 10″ springform pan first, and then press over the bottom of the pan.

BATTER

2 ounces sweet chocolate

2 pounds (4 8-ounce packages) cream cheese

1½ cups sugar

1 tablespoon raspberry extract

1½ teaspoons chocolate extract

pinch of salt

4 large eggs

1 cup fresh raspberries

Melt chocolate in the top of a double boiler over simmering water or in a microwave oven on half power, and reserve.

In a mixer, whip cream cheese on the highest speed for 5 minutes, then add sugar and whip for 2 minutes more. Add melted chocolate, extracts, and salt and blend together thoroughly. Add the eggs, one at a time, keeping the mixer on the lowest speed in order to prevent too much air from destroying the proper consistency of the batter; mix just until each egg has been incorporated into the batter. Fold in fresh raspberries carefully with a rubber spatula.

Pour batter into the crust and bake in a preheated oven for 55–60 minutes. Remove cake from oven and let stand on a countertop for 10 minutes while you prepare sour-cream glaze. This essential step allows the interior of the cake to solidify without overbaking or burning. Any cracks in the cake will be concealed under the sour-cream glaze.

SOUR-CREAM GLAZE

2 cups sour cream

¼ cup sugar

1 teaspoon raspberry liqueur

   shaved chocolate, as needed, for garnish

Combine sour cream, sugar, and raspberry liqueur with a rubber spatula in a plastic bowl. Spread evenly and smoothly over top of baked filling and return to 350 degree F. oven for 10 minutes. Remove from oven, sprinkle with shaved chocolate, and place **immediately** in refrigerator to cool. This prevents cracks from forming on top of the cake.

Before serving, let cheesecake stand at room temperature for 10 minutes to allow the butter in the crust to loosen its bond with the metal ring. When you release the springform clasp, the crust will generally detach naturally from the sides. If it sticks, separate crust from the sides gently with a metal spatula or a sharp knife.

Strawberry Cheesecake

Preheat oven to 350 degrees F. If ingredients are not at room temperature, add five minutes to baking time.

CRUST

¼ pound (1 stick) lightly salted butter

2 cups finely ground tea-biscuit crumbs

¼ cup sugar

Melt butter over very low heat. Combine butter with crumbs and sugar in a food processor until thoroughly blended or stir and mash together with a fork in a roomy bowl. Press small amounts of crust mix bit by bit all the way up the sides of an ungreased 10″ springform pan first, and then press over the bottom of the pan.

BATTER

1 pint fresh strawberries

1 tablespoon Fruit Fresh

2 pounds (4 8-ounce packages) cream cheese

2 cups sugar

1½ tablespoons strawberry liqueur

1 teaspoon strawberry extract

pinch of salt

4 large eggs

Save a few of the most beautiful strawberries to decorate the cake. Remove the stems from the rest, slice them, and sprinkle with Fruit Fresh to stop them from turning brown.

In a mixer, whip cream cheese on the highest speed for 5 minutes, then add sugar and whip for 2 minutes more. Add liqueur, extract, and salt and blend together thoroughly. Add the eggs, one at a time, keeping the mixer on the lowest speed in order to prevent too much air from destroying the proper consistency of the batter; mix just until each egg has been incorporated into the batter.

Pour batter into the crust, fold in sliced strawberries, and bake in a preheated oven for 1 hour. Remove cake from oven and let stand on a countertop for 10 minutes while you prepare sour-cream glaze. This essential step allows the interior of the cake to solidify without overbaking or burning. Any cracks in the cake will be concealed under the sour-cream glaze.

SOUR-CREAM GLAZE

- 2 cups sour cream
- ¼ cup sugar
- 1 teaspoon triple sec or strawberry liqueur
- reserved whole strawberries

Combine sour cream, sugar, and liqueur with a rubber spatula in a plastic bowl. Spread evenly and smoothly over top of baked filling and return to 350 degree F. oven for 10 minutes. Remove from oven and place **immediately** in refrigerator to cool. This prevents cracks from forming on top of the cake. When cool, garnish with reserved whole strawberries.

Before serving, let cheesecake stand at room temperature for 10 minutes to allow the butter in the crust to loosen its bond with the metal ring. When you release the springform clasp, the crust will generally detach naturally from the sides. If it sticks, separate crust from the sides gently with a metal spatula or a sharp knife.

Spicy Plum Cheesecake

Preheat oven to 350 degrees F. If ingredients are not at room temperature, add five minutes to baking time.

CRUST
- ¼ pound (1 stick) lightly salted butter
- 1½ cups finely ground vanilla-wafer crumbs
- ½ cup chopped pecans
- 1 teaspoon cinnamon
- ¼ cup sugar

Melt butter over very low heat. Combine butter with crumbs, pecans, cinnamon, and sugar in a food processor until thoroughly blended or stir and mash together with a fork in a roomy bowl. Press small amounts of crust mix bit by bit all the way up the sides of an ungreased 10″ springform pan first, and then press over the bottom of the pan.

BATTER
- 1 16-ounce can of purple plums
- ½ cup chopped pecans
- ½ teaspoon ground ginger
- ⅛ teaspoon cinnamon
- ⅛ teaspoon nutmeg
- 2 pounds (4 8-ounce packages) cream cheese
- 1½ cups sugar
- 1 tablespoon dark rum
- pinch of salt
- 4 large eggs

Drain, halve, and pit the plums. Save 4 halves for garnish and blot excess liquid from them with a paper towel. Slice the remaining plums, mix with nuts, ginger, cinnamon, and nutmeg and reserve.

In a mixer, whip cream cheese on the highest speed for 5 minutes, then add sugar and whip for 2 minutes more. Add rum and salt and blend together thoroughly. Add the eggs, one at a time, keeping the mixer on the lowest speed in order to prevent too much air from destroying the proper consistency of the batter; mix just until each egg has been incorporated into the batter. Fold in reserved sliced, spiced plums with a rubber spatula.

Pour batter into the crust and bake in a preheated oven for 1 hour and 10 minutes. Remove cake from oven and let stand on a countertop for 10 minutes while you prepare sour-cream glaze. This essential step allows the interior of the cake to solidify without overbaking or burning. Any cracks in the cake will be concealed under the sour-cream glaze.

SOUR-CREAM GLAZE

2 cups sour cream

¼ cup sugar

1 teaspoon dark rum

reserved plum halves, cut into slivers

½ cup coconut flakes

Combine sour cream, sugar, and rum with a rubber spatula in a plastic bowl. Spread evenly and smoothly over top of baked filling, garnish with plums, sprinkle with coconut, and return to 350 degree F. oven for 10 minutes. Remove from oven and place **immediately** in refrigerator to cool. This prevents cracks from forming on top of the cake.

Before serving, let cheesecake stand at room temperature for 10 minutes to allow the butter in the crust to loosen its bond with the metal ring. When you release the springform clasp, the crust will generally detach naturally from the sides. If it sticks, separate crust from the sides gently with a metal spatula or a sharp knife.

Cappuccino Swirl Cheesecake

Preheat oven to 350 degrees F. If ingredients are not at room temperature, add five minutes to baking time.

CRUST

- ¼ pound (1 stick) lightly salted butter
- 1 cup finely ground chocolate-wafer crumbs
- 1 cup finely ground vanilla-wafer crumbs
- 1 teaspoon coffee or mocha flavoring
- ¼ cup sugar

Melt butter over very low heat. Combine butter with crumbs, flavoring, and sugar in a food processor until thoroughly blended or stir and mash together with a fork in a roomy bowl. Press small amounts of crust mix bit by bit all the way up the sides of an ungreased 10″ springform pan first, and then press over the bottom of the pan.

BATTER

- 6 ounces coffee-flavored chocolate
- 2 pounds (4 8-ounce packages) cream cheese
- 1½ cups sugar
- 1 tablespoon dried cappuccino mix
- 1 teaspoon coffee or mocha extract
- 1½ teaspoons light rum
- pinch of salt
- 4 large eggs

Melt 4 ounces coffee-flavored chocolate in the top of a double boiler over simmering water or in a microwave oven on half power, and reserve. Coarsely chop the other 2 ounces of chocolate and reserve.

In a mixer, whip cream cheese on the highest speed for 5 minutes, then add sugar and whip for 2 minutes more. Add half of the melted chocolate, cappuccino mix, extract, rum, and salt and blend together thoroughly. Add the eggs, one at a time, keeping the mixer on the lowest speed in order to prevent too much air from destroying the proper consistency of the batter; mix just until each egg has been incorporated into the batter. Fold the chopped chocolate into the batter with a rubber spatula.

Pour batter into the crust, dribble remaining chocolate on it, swirl it into the batter with the tip of a knife, and bake in a preheated oven for 1 hour and 10 minutes. Remove cake from oven and let stand on a countertop for 10 minutes while you prepare sour-cream glaze. This essential step allows the interior of the cake to solidify without overbaking or burning. Any cracks in the cake will be concealed under the sour-cream glaze.

SOUR-CREAM GLAZE

2 cups sour cream

¼ cup sugar

1 teaspoon light rum

Combine sour cream, sugar, and rum with a rubber spatula in a plastic bowl. Spread evenly and smoothly over top of baked filling and return to 350 degree F. oven for 10 minutes. Remove from oven and place **immediately** in refrigerator to cool. This prevents cracks from forming on top of the cake.

Before serving, let cheesecake stand at room temperature for 10 minutes to allow the butter in the crust to loosen its bond with the metal ring. When you release the springform clasp, the crust will generally detach naturally from the sides. If it sticks, separate crust from the sides gently with a metal spatula or a sharp knife.

Pumpkin Nut Cheesecake

Preheat oven to 350 degrees F. If ingredients are not at room temperature, add five minutes to baking time.

CRUST

¼ pound (1 stick) lightly salted butter

1 cup finely ground vanilla-wafer crumbs

1 cup finely ground spiced-wafer crumbs

¼ cup chopped walnuts

¼ cup sugar

Melt butter over very low heat. Combine butter with crumbs, nuts, and sugar in a food processor until thoroughly blended or stir and mash together with a fork in a roomy bowl. Press small amounts of crust mix bit by bit all the way up the sides of an ungreased 10″ springform pan first, and then press over the bottom of the pan.

BATTER

1½ pounds (3 8-ounce packages) cream cheese

1½ cups sugar

½ cup maple syrup

1 cup canned pumpkin

1 teaspoon brandy

1½ tablespoons Irish Mist, rum, or Drambuie

1½ teaspoons cinnamon

¼ teaspoon mace

⅛ teaspoon nutmeg

½ cup chopped walnuts

1 ounce crystallized ginger, minced

pinch of salt

4 large eggs

In a mixer whip cream cheese on the highest speed for 5 minutes, then add sugar and whip for 2 minutes more. Add maple syrup, pumpkin, brandy, liqueur or rum, cinnamon, mace, nutmeg, walnuts, ginger, and salt and blend together thoroughly. Add the eggs, one at a time, keeping the mixer on the lowest speed in order to prevent too much air from destroying the proper consistency of the batter; mix just until each egg has been incorporated into the batter.

Pour batter into the crust and bake in a preheated oven for 1 hour and 10 minutes. Remove cake from oven and let stand on a countertop for 10 minutes. This essential step allows the interior of the cake to solidify without overbaking or burning. Refrigerate cake until almost ready to serve.

WHIPPED CREAM ROSETTE TOPPING
1 cup heavy cream
2 tablespoons confectioners' sugar
2 teaspoons cognac

Two hours before you are ready to serve cheesecake, put beaters and bowl of your mixer in the freezer for 10 minutes to chill. Whip cream until thick with an electric mixer. Add sugar and cognac and combine until blended. Fit a pastry bag with a star tube, fill with whipped cream and cover the top of the cake with rosettes, or if you have no pastry bag, just spread the whipped cream over the top of the cake. Remove from springform pan and refrigerate until ready to cut and serve.

Kosher for Passover Cheesecake

Preheat oven to 350 degrees F. If ingredients are not at room temperature, add five minutes to baking time.

CRUST

¼ pound (1 stick) lightly salted butter
1 cup finely ground kosher for Passover
    chocolate macaroon crumbs
1 cup chopped Brazil nuts
¼ cup sugar

Melt butter over very low heat. Combine butter with crumbs, nuts, and sugar in a food processor until thoroughly blended or stir and mash together with a fork in a roomy bowl. Press small amounts of crust mix bit by bit all the way up the sides of an ungreased 10″ springform pan first, and then press over the bottom of the pan.

BATTER

2 pounds (4 8-ounce packages) cream cheese
1½ cups sugar
1½ tablespoons fresh lemon juice
    pinch of salt
4 large eggs
½ cup chopped Brazil nuts

In a mixer, whip cream cheese on the highest speed for 5 minutes, then add sugar and whip for 2 minutes more. Add lemon juice and salt and blend together thoroughly. Add the eggs, one at a time, keeping the mixer on the lowest speed in order to prevent too much air from destroying the proper consistency of the batter; mix just until each egg has been incorporated into the batter. Fold in nuts with a rubber spatula.

Pour batter into the crust and bake in a preheated oven for 55–60 minutes. Remove cake from oven and let stand on a countertop for 10 minutes while you prepare sour-cream glaze. This essential step allows the interior of the

cake to solidify without overbaking or burning. Any cracks in the cake will be concealed under the sour-cream glaze.

SOUR-CREAM GLAZE

- 2 cups sour cream
- ¼ cup sugar
- 1 teaspoon vanilla extract
- 2 tablespoons grated lemon zest
- 2 tablespoons chopped Brazil nuts

Combine sour cream, sugar, and extract with a rubber spatula in a plastic bowl. Spread evenly and smoothly over top of baked filling and return to 350 degree F. oven for 10 minutes. Remove from oven, garnish with lemon zest and nuts, and place **immediately** in refrigerator to cool. This prevents cracks from forming on top of the cake.

Before serving, let cheesecake stand at room temperature for 10 minutes to allow the butter in the crust to loosen its bond with the metal ring. When you release the springform clasp, the crust will generally detach naturally from the sides. If it sticks, separate crust from the sides gently with a metal spatula or a sharp knife.

Nondairy Mandarin Orange Cheesecake

Preheat oven to 350 degrees F. If ingredients are not at room temperature, add five minutes to baking time.

CRUST

¼ pound (1 stick) margarine

2 cups finely ground crumbs from a cookie
      that's made only with oil

¼ cup sugar

Melt butter over very low heat. Combine butter with crumbs and sugar in a food processor until thoroughly blended or stir and mash together with a fork in a roomy bowl. Press small amounts of crust mix bit by bit all the way up the sides of an ungreased 10″ springform pan first, and then press over the bottom of the pan.

BATTER

2 pounds imitation cream cheese made from
      tofu

1½ cups sugar

1 tablespoon undiluted frozen orange juice

1½ teaspoons orange extract
      pinch of salt

4 large eggs

1 8-ounce can mandarin orange slices, drained
      and blotted with paper towels

In a mixer, whip cream cheese on the highest speed for 5 minutes, then add sugar and whip for 2 minutes more. Add orange juice, extract, and salt and blend together thoroughly. Add the eggs, one at a time, keeping the mixer on the lowest speed in order to prevent too much air from destroying the proper consistency of the batter; mix just until each egg has been incorporated into the batter. Save 12 orange slices for garnish and fold the remaining orange slices into the batter with a rubber spatula.

Pour batter into the crust and bake in a preheated oven for 1 hour. Remove cake from oven and let stand on a countertop for 10 minutes while you prepare whipped creamer topping. This essential step allows the interior of the cake to solidify without overbaking or burning. Any cracks in the cake will be concealed under the topping.

WHIPPED CREAMER TOPPING

1 cup nondairy vanilla-flavored creamer

2 tablespoons confectioners' sugar

2 teaspoons cognac

About 2 hours before you are ready to serve the cheesecake, put mixer beaters in the freezer for 10 minutes to chill. Whip creamer until thick in an electric mixer. Add sugar and cognac and continue beating until they are blended in.

Fit a pastry bag with a star tube, fill with whipped creamer, and cover top of cake with rosettes. Return cake to refrigerator until ready to serve.

Before serving, let cheesecake stand at room temperature for 10 minutes to allow the margarine in the crust to loosen its bond with the metal ring. When you release the springform clasp, the crust will generally detach naturally from the sides. If it sticks, separate crust from the sides gently with a metal spatula or a sharp knife.

Chocolate Surprise Cheesecake

Preheat oven to 350 degrees F. If ingredients are not at room temperature, add five minutes to baking time.

CRUST

- ¼ pound (1 stick) lightly salted butter
- 1 cup finely ground chocolate-wafer crumbs
- 1 cup chopped walnuts
- ¼ cup sugar

Melt butter over very low heat. Combine butter with crumbs, nuts, and sugar in a food processor until thoroughly blended or stir and mash together with a fork in a roomy bowl. Press small amounts of crust mix bit by bit all the way up the sides of an ungreased 10″ springform pan first, and then press over the bottom of the pan.

BATTER

- 5 ounces dark chocolate or chocolate chips— 3 ounces to be melted, 2 ounces to be blended as is into the batter
- 5 ounces peanut-butter bits—3 ounces to be melted, 2 ounces to be blended as is into the batter
- 2 pounds (4 8-ounce packages) cream cheese
- 1½ cups sugar
- 1½ tablespoons rum
- pinch of salt
- 4 large eggs

Melt 3 ounces each of the dark chocolate and peanut-butter bits separately over simmering water or in a microwave on half power, and reserve each.

In a mixer, whip cream cheese on the highest speed for 5 minutes, then add sugar and whip for 2 minutes more. Add rum and salt and blend together thoroughly. Add the eggs, one at a time, keeping the mixer on the lowest speed in order to prevent too much air from destroying the proper consistency of the batter; mix just until each egg has been incorporated into the batter. Remove 2 cups of batter and reserve.

To the remaining batter in the processor or mixer, add the melted peanut-butter bits and process until well combined. Fold in whole peanut-butter bits and pour batter into the springform pan.

Without cleaning the processor or mixer bowl, add the reserved cups of batter and the melted chocolate, and combine well. Then fold in the chocolate chips. The chocolate batter can be spread on top of the peanut-butter batter in the springform pan, or it can be cut in to achieve a marble effect.

Bake in a preheated oven for 40–45 minutes. Remove cake from oven and let stand on a countertop for 10 minutes while you prepare sour-cream glaze. This essential step allows the interior of the cake to solidify without overbaking or burning. Any cracks in the cake will be concealed under the sour-cream glaze.

SOUR-CREAM GLAZE

    2 cups sour cream
    ¼ cup sugar
    1 teaspoon rum
    1 ounce chocolate, melted
    1 ounce peanut-butter bits, melted

Combine sour cream, sugar, and rum with a rubber spatula in a plastic bowl. Spread evenly and smoothly over top of baked filling and return to 350 degree F. oven for 10 minutes. Remove from oven and drizzle melted chocolate and peanut-butter bits on the crust, and place in refrigerator immediately to cool.

Before serving, let cheesecake stand at room temperature for 10 minutes to allow the butter in the crust to loosen its bond with the metal ring. When you release the springform clasp, the crust will generally detach naturally from the sides. If it sticks, separate crust from the sides gently with a metal spatula or a sharp knife.

Strawberry-Rhubarb Cheesecake

Preheat oven to 350 degrees F. If ingredients are not at room temperature, add five minutes to baking time.

PRELIMINARY

1 pound frozen rhubarb
¼ cup water
¾ cup sugar

Boil water and rhubarb together for 5 minutes, then add sugar and simmer, covered, for 20 minutes more. During this time, you can make your crust and prepare most of your batter.

CRUST

¼ pound (1 stick) lightly salted butter
1 cup finely ground almond-flavored cookie
   crumbs
1 cup chopped pine nuts
¼ cup sugar

Melt butter over very low heat. Combine butter with crumbs, nuts, and sugar in a food processor until thoroughly blended or stir and mash together with a fork in a roomy bowl. Press small amounts of crust mix bit by bit all the way up the sides of an ungreased 10″ springform pan first, and then press over the bottom of the pan.

BATTER

2 pounds (4 8-ounce packages) cream cheese
1½ cups sugar
1½ tablespoons strawberry liqueur or flavoring
   pinch of salt
4 large eggs

In a mixer, whip cream cheese on the highest speed for 5 minutes, then add sugar and whip for 2 minutes more. Add liqueur or flavoring, salt, and blend together thoroughly. Add the eggs, one at a time, keeping the mixer on the lowest speed in order to prevent too much air from destroying the proper consistency of the batter; mix just until each egg has been incorporated into the batter. Drain rhubarb and fold into the batter. Pour batter into springform pan.

Bake in a preheated oven for 40–45 minutes. Remove cake from oven and let stand on a countertop for 10 minutes while you prepare sour-cream glaze. This essential step allows the interior of the cake to solidify without overbaking or burning. Any cracks in the cake will be concealed under the sour-cream glaze.

SOUR-CREAM GLAZE

2 cups sour cream

¼ cup sugar

1 teaspoon almond extract

Combine sour cream, sugar, and extract with a rubber spatula in a plastic bowl. Spread evenly and smoothly over top of baked filling and return to 350 degree F. oven for 10 minutes. Remove from oven and place in refrigerator **immediately** to cool.

Before serving, let cheesecake stand at room temperature for 10 minutes to allow the butter in the crust to loosen its bond with the metal ring. When you release the springform clasp, the crust will generally detach naturally from the sides. If it sticks, separate crust from the sides gently with a metal spatula or a sharp knife.

GARNISH

1 pint of fresh strawberries whole or sliced,
    sprinkled with Fruit Fresh to keep them from
    turning brown

Just before serving garnish with strawberries.

Savory Smoked Salmon, Dill, Chive Cheesecake

Preheat oven to 350 degrees F. Ingredients need not be at room temperature. If they are not at room temperature, add five minutes to baking time.

CRUST

- 3 cups finely ground fresh focaccia breadcrumbs
- ¼ pound (1 stick) lightly salted butter

Melt butter over very low heat. Combine butter with crumbs in a food processor until thoroughly blended or stir and mash together with a fork in a roomy bowl. Press small amounts of crust mix bit by bit all the way up the sides of an ungreased 10″ springform pan first and then press over the bottom of the pan.

BATTER

- 2 pounds (4 8-ounce packages) cream cheese
- 4 ounces smoked salmon, cut into thin slivers
- 1 ounce fresh dill, finely snipped
- 1 ounce fresh chives, finely snipped
- 1 tablespoon lemon or lime juice
- 4 large eggs
- 1 ounce sundried tomatoes, finely sliced
- 10 thin asparagus, grilled and cut into 1-inch chunks
- 5 scallions including 3 inches of greens, grilled and cut into 1-inch chunks

In a mixer whip cream cheese on the highest speed for 5 minutes, add smoked salmon, dill, and chives and blend together thoroughly. Add the eggs, one at a time, keeping the mixer and juice on the lowest speed in order to prevent too much air from destroying the proper consistency of the batter;

mix just until each egg has been incorporated into the batter. Fold in tomatoes, asparagus, and scallions. Pour batter into springform pan.

NOTE: If you use a food processor, blend together cream cheese, smoked salmon, dill, chives, and lemon or lime juice. Add the eggs one at a time until they are just incorporated into the batter. By hand, fold in tomatoes, asparagus, and scallions and pour into springform pan.

Bake in a preheated oven for 40 minutes. Remove cake from oven and let stand on a countertop for 10 minutes while you prepare sour-cream glaze. This essential step allows the interior of the cake to solidify without overbaking or burning. Any cracks in the cake will be concealed under the sour-cream glaze.

SOUR-CREAM GLAZE

2 cups sour cream

¼ cup snipped dill and/or chives

sprigs of dill for garnish

Combine snipped dill and/or chives with the sour cream with a rubber spatula in a plastic bowl. Spread evenly and smoothly over top of baked filling and return to 350 degree F. oven for 10 minutes. Remove from oven and place in refrigerator immediately to cool. Just before serving garnish with sprigs of dill.

Before serving, let cheesecake stand at room temperature for 10 minutes to allow the butter in the crust to loosen its bond with the metal ring. When you release the springform clasp, the crust will generally detach naturally from the sides. If it sticks, separate crust from the sides gently with a metal spatula or a sharp knife.

BONUS!

The Magic Formula Which Will Allow You to Experiment and Concoct Your Own Personally Flavored Baked Cheesecakes

So what do you do if there's a flavor of your own that you want to try? Make it yourself, using the following magic basic formula:

Preheat oven to 350 degrees F. If ingredients are not at room temperature, add five minutes to baking time.

CRUST

¼ pound (1 stick) lightly salted butter

2 cups finely ground dry ingredients, either
finely ground cookie crumbs, chopped nuts,
or a combination of finely ground cookie
crumbs and chopped nuts

¼ cup sugar

1 teaspoon flavoring, liqueur, or extract
(optional)

Melt butter over very low heat. Combine butter with crumbs/nuts or both and sugar in a food processor until thoroughly blended or stir and mash together with a fork in a roomy bowl. Press small amounts of crust mix bit by bit all the way up the sides of an ungreased 10″ springform pan first, and then press over the bottom of the pan.

BATTER

2 pounds (4 8-ounce packages) cream cheese

1½ cups sugar

1½ tablespoons flavoring, extract, liqueur, or juice

pinch of salt

4 large eggs

various forms of chocolate, flavored chips,
or dried or fresh fruits (optional)

In a mixer, whip cream cheese on the highest speed for 5 minutes, then add sugar and whip for 2 minutes more. Add flavoring, extract, liqueur or juice, and salt, and blend together thoroughly. Add the eggs, one at a time, keeping the mixer on the lowest speed in order to prevent too much air from destroying the proper consistency of the batter; mix just until each egg has been incorporated into the batter.

NOTE: If you use a food processor to prepare the batter, blend the ingredients well and add the eggs one at a time until they are just incorporated into the batter.

Notes Regarding Optional Added Items

VARIOUS FORMS OF CHOCOLATE OR FLAVORED CHIPS: If you wish to incorporate them into the batter, melt them in a double boiler over simmering water or in a microwave oven at half power and reserve. Incorporate them into the batter as a final step, right before batter is poured into springform pan.

DRIED FRUITS: Cut into very thin slivers and soak in liqueur, brandy, or rum to soften, then fold into the batter at the very end, right before batter is poured into springform pan.

FRESH FRUITS: Cut into small pieces and fold into the batter at the very end, right before batter is poured into springform pan.

Bake in a preheated oven for 50–55 minutes. Remove cake from oven and let stand on a countertop for 10 minutes while you prepare sour-cream glaze. This essential step allows the interior of the cake to solidify without overbaking or burning. Any cracks in the cake will be concealed under the sour-cream glaze.

SOUR-CREAM GLAZE

- 2 cups sour cream
- ¼ cup sugar
- 1 teaspoon almond or any other extract

Combine sour cream, sugar, and extract with a rubber spatula in a plastic bowl. Spread evenly and smoothly over top of baked filling, and return to 350 degree F. oven for 10 minutes. Remove from oven and place **immediately** in refrigerator to cool. This prevents cracks from forming on top of the cake.

Before serving, let cheesecake stand at room temperature for 10 minutes to allow the butter in the crust to loosen its bond with the metal ring. When you release the springform clasp, the crust will generally detach naturally from the sides. If it sticks, separate crust from the sides gently with a metal spatula or a sharp knife.

GARNISHES

Garnishes should be arranged in an attractive pattern on sour-cream glaze just before cake is ready to be served. Slices of fresh fruit should be sprinkled with Fruit Fresh to keep them from turning brown.

WORDS OF WISDOM ABOUT
NONBAKED CHEESECAKES

READ BEFORE MAKING!

*W*e always thought great nonbaked cheesecakes were an impossible dream, and for good reason. Most of the recipes we'd seen previously were so complicated that we always found it easier to pop one of our regular cakes into the oven.

So how come we undertook nonbakes?

Somebody made Myra an offer she couldn't refuse. National TV host Gary Collins asked her to develop a cheesecake that required no baking for a holiday cooking segment on *Hour Detroit* magazine, his syndicated show. She didn't think it was wise or prudent to say no to Gary without giving his request the old high school try. So Myra put on her thinking cap and went into her kitchen, and when she came out a week later, there were several tasty unbaked cheesecakes in her refrigerator. Gary Collins had asked for only one cake, but Myra's family motto has always been, "More is better!"

These bakeless wonders were creamy and flavorful. Most of the original testers even thought they tasted baked. Gary Collins loved them. So did the hosts of four or five other New York, Los Angeles, and Philadelphia TV shows. Myra's nonbaked pumpkin cheesecake even won the heart of one of America's greatest kvetches, the late Howard Cosell, who told Gary on national TV that he'd always hated anything made with pumpkin until he tasted Myra's instant pumpkin cheesecake. Don't believe us? Ask Myra to send you a copy of the tape.

Everyone was astonished to learn how quickly and easily any one of these nonbaked cheesecakes could be whipped up in a food processor, and a record-breaking number of viewers who watched her do it called in requesting recipes. To answer any of your inquiries, either culinary or philosophical, about nonbaked cheesecake, we're going to play question-and-answer. If you think you've discovered a question Myra hasn't answered, don't trouble yourself too much. Anything she's omitted isn't worth knowing. Believe me, she measured the ingredients, weighed them, chopped them, whisked them, and mashed them—and when she says something doesn't work, better believe it's true.

Why Is Melting Chocolate Like Love?

Because, as the song says, you can't hurry it. No matter which method you use, chocolate melts best slowly. If you're using a Flame Tamer (a metal circle with holes in it which conducts the heat into the bottom of the pan indirectly, so the pan really works just like a double boiler), keep the burner underneath it on low heat. If you're using a double boiler, the water in the bottom pot should be simmering, not erupting. If you're using a microwave, use it only on half power. High power either burns the chocolate or burns the butter. Melt the chocolate alone first on two 20-second segments at half power. Then add butter, and zap butter and partially melted chocolate on half power for 10 seconds at a time, checking the chocolate frequently to see if it melted. And don't melt the chocolate in the microwave in a teacup. The container that holds it should be big enough to hold all the crumbs and nuts in the crust as well. Incidentally, dark chocolate melts faster and more easily than white chocolate and/or butterscotch-flavored or peanut-butter chips.

How Are These Nonbaked Cheesecakes
Different from Most Other Nonbaked Cheesecakes?

Most traditional nonbaked cheesecakes contain (ugh!) gelatin. Call us picky, but gelatin always reminds us of childhood afflictions. Every time either one of us had a communicable disease, our mothers would appear at our bedsides bearing squares of Jell-O riddled with canned fruit cocktail. Even as tykes, we both disliked the taste of gelatin and absolutely hated its appearance and texture. Making gelatin is a pill. It has to be softened in liquid and then dissolved over low heat. Many gelatin-based nonbaked cheesecakes also require that you separate eggs and whip up egg whites. Not only does that mean extra prep work, it means a messed-up kitchen filled with mucho dirty pans—a double minus, especially if you're pressed for time like most of are all of the time. Today's cooks have more interesting uses for their spare time than scrubbing pots.

How Do Our Unbaked Cheesecakes
Prevent Dishpan Hands?

These cakes require ONE PAN for melting butter and some form of chocolate, ONE FOOD PROCESSOR for grinding cookies into crumbs and/or chopping nuts and blending batter, ONE KNIFE for cutting whatever needs to be cut, ONE FORK for blending the crumb crust, ONE RUBBER SPATULA, which does pretty much anything else, ONE OPTIONAL WHISK, and ONE ROLL OF PAPER TOWELS for wiping most of the bowls.

How Can You Use a Food Processor to Make Crusts
and Batter Without Having to Wash the Bowl Every Time?

Let's start with the crusts. The chocolate and butter are melted together in a double boiler, a microwave oven, or a frying pan over a Flame Tamer. No matter which method you choose, the melting bowl or pan does double duty as your crust-mixing bowl. Just dump all your other crust ingredients in the melted butter/chocolate blend all at once and combine them by mashing them together with an ordinary fork. That saves washing a mixing bowl. You just have to wipe it out with a paper towel. You can even use the plastic bowl of your food processor as a melting pan in a microwave oven, and throw in the cookies and nuts and whiz them together. Then simply wipe out the bowl of your processor and your blade with a paper towel—may the recyclers forgive me!—and dispose of it, and your food processor is ready to cream the daylights out of your batter without any interim washing at all.

What If Your Filling and Crust Require Two Different Kinds of Melted Chocolate?

Melt each kind in a different container, mix each with half of the dry ingredients, and then wipe both contaners out with paper towels.

What Do You Mean by "Medium-Fine Chopped Nuts"?

You really have to watch the nuts when you're chopping them. If they're too big, they'll make the crust too chunky, and if they're too fine, they turn into nut butters and make the crust too mushy.

The best way to chop nuts for these crusts is to process them for 30 seconds and then pulse on-off 15 to 20 times, checking the texture often and stirring the nuts around to make sure that they are fluffy. Since we want them medium fine, you must stop chopping before they turn into nut butters. Hard nuts like almonds chop up easily. Softer nuts like macadamia and pine nuts have to be watched carefully because they mush up very easily. If they turn to mush, you can still use them—but next time, if you want the proper texture in your crusts, stop chopping a little sooner. Do it a few times, and you'll get the knack.

Chopping nuts and cookies together in a food processor produces the best results because the cookie crumbs absorb the excess nut oils and prevent the nuts from turning mushy.

Why Don't These Unbaked Crusts Require Baking?

These crusts are independent and substantial as is. The cohesive element in these unbaked crusts is the melted chocolate which, when it chills, transforms all the other crust ingredients into a delicious candy shell.

Why Doesn't This Batter Need to Be Baked?

The acidic juices that come in contact with the sweetened condensed milk alter the protein in the milk so that it soaks up liquid, which sets the batter. The process works best with fresh lime and lemon juice, but other citrus juices will work if their acid content is boosted. That why we never dilute any of the frozen concentrated juices used in these nonbaked cakes, and why we increase the acidity by adding Fruit Fresh to the batter. Fruit Fresh is sweet, but otherwise flavorless, and high in ascorbic acid. It's a fruit protector; its main ingredients are dextrose (corn sugar) and ascorbic acid (vitamin C). The other ingredient that sets the nonbaked batters is melted chocolate, which hardens when it chills.

What Kind of Pan Works Best for the Nonbaked Cakes?

We prefer a 10-inch springform pan because these cakes look and cut better when they are wide and flat, rather than small and high. That means the crusts should not go higher than 1½ inches up the sides of the springform. On many of these cakes, 1 inch is sufficient. The lower the crusts on the side are, the thicker they can be. A more substantial crust supports the unbaked batter best.

How Should the Nonbaked Cheesecakes Be Cut and Served?

Because these nonbaked cheesecakes are rich and sweet, small portions—flat, narrow wedges—are really enough for most folks. On the other hand, four-star gluttons can and usually will ask for seconds.

Suppose I Don't Have Any Springform Pans?

Get one. Even better, buy several. They cost next to nothing. We've found them in supermarkets for as little as $6. If you don't have any, you can use a pie pan or even an 8-inch throwaway aluminum baking pan.

Why Can't I Use a Store-Bought Crumb Crust?

They don't hold together well. Besides, they always taste like they contain medicated skin cream for shortening.

How Long Will It Take for the Nonbaked Cheesecakes to Set?

Many of these nonbaked cheesecakes will set after two hours of refrigeration, but they are best if they are left in the refrigerator overnight to firm up and meld their flavors. These nonbaked cheesecakes are generally more custard-like than baked cheesecakes, but nonbakes will firm up nicely after two days of refrigeration, or a few hours in the freezer. As a rule of thumb, the longer the nonbaked cheesecakes set in the refrigerator, the more solid they become, because the chemical processes that set them continue to work during that time.

How Long Will the Nonbaked Cheesecakes Keep?

They can remain in the refrigerator for a week. We've kept them there for two weeks, and nobody ever got sick or complained. They also freeze nicely. They hold up better and longer than baked cheesecakes because they have no topping. It's the topping that discolors and makes a cheesecake that's been refrigerated too long look unappetizing and unappealing.

Do the Nonbaked Cheesecakes Have to Be
Made on a Metal or a Cardboard Foil-Wrapped Bottom?

No. Make them on a plain uncovered cardboard round in a springform pan.

How Fussy Do I Have to Be About the Ingredients?

Very fussy indeed. Because there are no mitigating factors, as in baking, the quality of the ingredients is crucial. Try to avoid artificial flavorings. Even the best of these sometimes have a slightly bitter aftertaste.

Avoid no-frills cream cheese. Store brands are usually saltier, gummier, and overly stabilized. But when it comes to sweetened condensed milk, they all taste and act pretty much alike, so buy the cheapest one.

Can I Use a Lower-Calorie Cheese and
Still Get as Delicious a Nonbaked Cake?

There's very little difference between the taste of light and regular cream cheese. The light cream cheese has 20 fewer calories per ounce, or 320 fewer calories per cake. On the other hand, if you cut the cheesecake in smaller slices, each slice will have fewer calories—not significant in the grand scheme of weight reduction. You can use a lower-calorie cheese and still make an instant cheesecake. We'll show you how in Chapter 10.

What! No Toppings or Glazes?

As we've said before, bakers designed toppings and glazes for the same reason chefs created sauces: to hide a multitude of sins, like burns, cracks, and carbuncles of undissolved cream cheese. Nonbaked cheesecakes never crack or burn and the food processor makes the batter smooth and silky, so there's no need to cover or hide anything.

Suppose I Want to Make a
Smaller Nonbaked Cheesecake?

Use half the ingredients and a smaller 8-inch springform pan.

What If I Can't Find a Particular Kind of Nut or Cookie?

Use whatever nut or cookie you happen to have on hand.

Why Can't I Use Chocolate Chips?

You can!

How Should a Nonbaked Cheesecake Be Stored?

If you plan to serve it within a week, keep it in the springform pan, and keep it refrigerated, in a box, or covered with a cardboard round. Otherwise, freeze it in the springform pan, wrapped tightly in aluminum foil. Once it's frozen, the cake can be removed from the springform pan and kept in the freezer in a cardboard cake box.

How Long Should Nonbaked Cheesecakes
Sit at Room Temperature Before Serving?

No more than 15 minutes, just long enough to let the butter in the crust warm a little and release its bond to the metal ring. This will allow you to remove the cake from the springform pan more easily. Nonbaked cheesecakes should be served cold. They can even be cut, served, and eaten frozen.

Any Last Helpful Hints?

If you find the crust mix very greasy, press it against the sides of the springform pan with a fork. Otherwise, wrap your fingers in plastic wrap like a mitten, and use your wrapped fingers to press, smooth, and flatten walnut-sized nuggets of crust mix against the side of the pan. A sheet of plastic wrap will help you make sure the crust mix covers the bottom, too. Cover any empty spaces in the bottom with plastic wrap, and then run your fingertips, your knuckles, or the back of a spoon over the area to spread the crust mix better.

NONBAKED CHEESECAKE RECIPES

Basic Lime-Almond Nonbaked Cheesecake

CRUST

- 3 tablespoons lightly salted butter
- 4 ounces white chocolate
- 1 teaspoon almond extract
- ¾ cup finely ground vanilla-wafer crumbs
- ¾ cup almonds, chopped medium fine

Melt butter and white chocolate over simmering water in the top of a double boiler or in food-processor bowl—or another small plastic or glass bowl—in a microwave oven at half power. When melted, whisk into a smooth, even mass. Measure crumbs and nuts into the food-processor bowl, add the melted chocolate mixture, and process for 5-second intervals, checking texture frequently. It should be fine and dry, rather than mushy. Using walnut-sized nuggets of crust mix, press them no more than 1½ inches up the sides of a 10″ springform pan with your fingers. Wrapping your hand in plastic will give you better control and keep the mix from sticking to your fingers. Press and smooth down the remainder of the crust mix over the bottom of the spring-form pan with your fingers or the back of a soup spoon. If there are empty spaces in the bottom crust, press the sides a bit thinner and use the excess to fill in the holes in the bottom, or just sprinkle some more cookie crumbs in the holes. Put the pan in the refrigerator to allow the crust to set.

FILLING
1 pound (2 8-ounce packages) cream cheese,
    each package cut into 8 squares
1 14-ounce can sweetened condensed milk
⅓ cup lime juice

In a mixer or food processor, whip cream cheese, condensed milk, and fla-voring together until creamy and well blended. Pour into crust. Spread the fill-ing around carefully with a rubber spatula so that it's level and adheres to the sides of the crust.

GARNISH
grated lime zest

Sprinkle lime zest on the top of the cake. Place in the refrigerator to set until ready to serve.

Before serving, let cheesecake stand at room temperature for 10–15 min-utes to allow the butter in the crust to loosen its bond with the metal ring. When you release the springform clasp, the crust will generally detach natu-rally from the sides. If it sticks, separate crust from the pan by inserting a metal spatula or sharp knife..

Luscious Lemon Nut Nonbaked Cheesecake

CRUST

3 tablespoons butter

4 ounces white chocolate

½ teaspoon lemon extract

1½ cups blanched almonds, chopped medium
     fine

Melt butter and white chocolate over simmering water in the top of a double boiler or in food-processor bowl—or in another small plastic or glass bowl—in a microwave oven at half power. When melted, whisk into a smooth, even mass. Measure nuts into the food-processor bowl, add extract and the melted chocolate mixture, and process for 5-second intervals, checking texture frequently. It should be fine and dry, rather than mushy. Using walnut-sized nuggets of crust mix, press them no more than 1½ inches up the sides of a 10″ springform pan with your fingers. Wrapping your hand in plastic will give you better control and keep the mix from sticking to your fingers. Press and smooth down the remainder of the crust mix over the bottom of the springform pan with your fingers or the back of a soup spoon. If there are empty spaces in the bottom crust, press the sides a bit thinner and use the excess to fill in the holes in the bottom, or just sprinkle some more cookie crumbs in the holes. Put the pan in the refrigerator to allow the crust to set.

FILLING

1 pound (2 8-ounce packages) cream cheese,
    each package cut into 8 squares

1 14-ounce can sweetened condensed milk

⅓ cup lemon juice

¾ teaspoon lemon extract

½ cup lemon curd

In a mixer or food processor, whip cream cheese, condensed milk, and lemon juice and lemon extract together until creamy and well blended. Pour into crust. Spread the filling around carefully with a rubber spatula so that it's level and adheres to the sides of the crust. Cut the lemon curd into the batter with the point of a knife to achieve a swirl pattern.

GARNISH

lemon curd (optional)

Spread a thin layer of bottled lemon curd over the top of the batter.

Before serving, let cheesecake stand at room temperature for 10–15 minutes to allow the butter in the crust to loosen its bond with the metal ring. When you release the springform clasp, the crust will generally detach naturally from the sides. If it sticks, separate crust from the pan by inserting a metal spatula or sharp knife.

Triple Chocolate Nonbaked Cheesecake

CRUST

3 tablespoons butter

2 ounces white chocolate

2 ounces dark chocolate, sweet or semisweet

½ cup finely ground vanilla-wafer crumbs

½ cup finely ground chocolate-wafer crumbs

½ cup chopped Brazil nuts

Melt butter and both chocolates over simmering water in the top of a double boiler or in food-processor bowl—or in another small plastic or glass bowl—in a microwave oven at half power. When melted, whisk into a smooth, even mass. Measure crumbs and nuts into the food-processor bowl, add the melted chocolate mixture, and process for 5-second intervals, checking texture frequently. It should be fine and dry, rather than mushy. Using walnut-sized nuggets of crust mix, press them no more than 1½ inches up the sides of a 10″ springform pan with your fingers. Wrapping your hand in plastic will give you better control and keep the mix from sticking to your fingers. Press and smooth down the remainder of the crust mix over the bottom of the springform pan with your fingers or the back of a soup spoon. If there are empty spaces in the bottom crust, press the sides a bit thinner and use the excess to fill in the blanks in the bottom, or just sprinkle some more cookie crumbs around the holes. Put the pan in the refrigerator to allow the crust to set.

FILLING

4 ounces dark chocolate, sweet or semisweet

1 pound (2 8-ounce packages) cream cheese,
   each package cut into 8 squares

1 14-ounce can sweetened condensed milk

2 teaspoons Fruit Fresh

⅓ cup frozen orange juice concentrate, undiluted

1½ tablespoons fresh lemon juice

1 tablespoon Grand Marnier

⅓ cup mini–chocolate chips

Melt chocolate as above and reserve. In a mixer or food processor, whip cream cheese, condensed milk, and melted chocolate together until creamy and well blended. Dissolve Fruit Fresh in juices and Grand Marnier, add with melted chocolate to batter, and process until well combined. Fold in chocolate chips with a rubber spatula and pour into crust.

Spread the filling around carefully with a rubber spatula so that it's level and adheres to the sides of the crust.

GARNISH

2 ounces dark chocolate

Melt an additional 2 ounces of chocolate and drizzle it on the top of the cake. Place in the refrigerator to set until ready to serve.

Before serving, let cheesecake stand at room temperature for 10–15 minutes to allow the butter in the crust to loosen its bond with the metal ring. When you release the springform clasp, the crust will generally detach naturally from the sides. If it sticks, separate crust from the pan by inserting a metal spatula or sharp knife.

Chocolate Surprise Nonbaked Cheesecake

CRUST

3   tablespoons butter

4   ounces peanut-butter bits

¾   cup finely ground chocolate-wafer crumbs

¾   cup peanuts, chopped medium fine

Melt butter and peanut-butter bits over simmering water in the top of a double boiler or in food-processor bowl—or in another small plastic or glass bowl—in a microwave oven at half power. When melted, whisk into a smooth, even mass. Measure crumbs and nuts into the food-processor bowl, add the melted chocolate mixture, and process for 5-second intervals, checking texture frequently. It should be fine and dry, rather than mushy. Using walnut-sized nuggets of crust mix, press them no more than 1½ inches up the sides of a 10″ springform pan with your fingers. Wrapping your hand in plastic will give you better control and keep the mix from sticking to your fingers. Press and smooth down the remainder of the crust mix over the bottom of the springform pan with your fingers or the back of a soup spoon. If there are empty spaces in the bottom crust, press the sides a bit thinner and use the excess to fill in the holes in the bottom, or just sprinkle some more cookie crumbs into the holes. Put the pan in the refrigerator to allow the crust to set.

FILLING

6   ounces peanut-butter bits, separated into
      4-ounce and 2-ounce quantities

2   ounces dark chocolate, sweet or semisweet

1   pound (2 8-ounce packages) cream cheese,
      each package cut into 8 squares

1   14-ounce can sweetened condensed milk

2   teaspoons Fruit Fresh

2   tablespoons lemon juice

Melt 4 ounces of peanut-butter bits and chocolate separately over simmering water in the top of a double boiler or in a small plastic bowl in a microwave oven on half power, and reserve each. In a mixer or food processor, whip cream cheese and condensed milk together until creamy and well blended. Remove one cup of batter and reserve. Dissolve Fruit Fresh in lemon juice and add with melted peanut-butter chips to batter in processor and process until well combined. Fold remaining peanut-butter bits into the peanut-butter batter in the processor bowl. Pour into crust. Mix remaining cup of batter with melted dark chocolate. Spread the chocolate batter evenly over the peanut-butter batter with a metal spatula or knife. The top should look as if the cake is solid chocolate, so the peanut-butter interior comes as a delightful surprise.

GARNISH
2 ounces dark chocolate, melted

Drizzle melted chocolate on top of the cake and put in the refrigerator to set.

Before serving, let cheesecake stand at room temperature for 10–15 minutes to allow the butter in the crust to loosen its bond with the metal ring. When you release the springform clasp, the crust will generally detach naturally from the sides. If it sticks, separate crust from the pan by inserting a metal spatula or sharp knife.

Nonbaked Double-Mint Cheesecake

CRUST

3 tablespoons butter

1 ounce white chocolate

3 ounces mint-flavored chocolate

¼ cup finely ground chocolate-wafer crumbs

½ cup finely ground vanilla-wafer crumbs

¾ cup pine nuts, chopped medium fine

Melt butter and both chocolates together over simmering water in the top of a double boiler or in food-processor bowl—or in another small plastic or glass bowl—in a microwave oven at half power. When melted, whisk into a smooth, even mass. Measure crumbs and nuts into the food processor bowl, add the melted chocolate mixture, and process for 5-second intervals, checking texture frequently. It should be fine and dry, rather than mushy. Using walnut-sized nuggets of crust mix, press them no more than 1½ inches up the sides of a 10″ springform pan with your fingers. Wrapping your hand in plastic will give you better control and keep the mix from sticking to your fingers. Press and smooth down the remainder of the crust mix over the bottom of the springform pan with your fingers or the back of a soup spoon. If there are empty spaces in the bottom crust, press the sides a bit thinner and use the excess to fill in the blanks in the bottom, or just sprinkle some more cookie crumbs in the holes. Put the pan in the refrigerator to allow the crust to harden and set.

FILLING

4 ounces mint-flavored chocolate

1 pound (2 8-ounce packages) cream cheese, each package cut into 8 squares

1 14-ounce can sweetened condensed milk

3 tablespoons Fruit Fresh

2 tablespoons lime juice

2 tablespoons white crème de menthe

1 teaspoon mint extract

¼ cup mint-flavored chocolate chips or
chocolate-covered mint patties, diced

Melt chocolate over simmering water in the top of a double boiler or in a microwave oven on half power, and reserve. In a mixer or food processor, whip cream cheese and condensed milk together until creamy and well blended. Dissolve Fruit Fresh in juice, crème de menthe, and mint extract; add to batter along with melted chocolate; and process until well combined. Fold in mint-flavored chips or diced mint patties and pour into crust. Spread the filling around carefully with a rubber spatula so that it's level and adheres to the sides of the crust.

GARNISH
chocolate-covered peppermint patties
one sprig of fresh mint

Cut mint patties into thin slivers and place around the cake like the numbers of a clock, insert the mint in the center, and put the cake in the refrigerator to set.

Before serving, let cheesecake stand at room temperature for 10–15 minutes to allow the butter in the crust to loosen its bond with the metal ring. When you release the springform clasp, the crust will generally detach naturally from the sides. If it sticks, separate crust from the pan by inserting a metal spatula or sharp knife.

Nonbaked Espresso Swirl Cheesecake

CRUST

3 tablespoons butter

4 ounces white chocolate

2 teaspoons instant espresso

1 tablespoon coffee extract

1 teaspoon coffee liqueur

¾ cup finely ground vanilla-wafer crumbs

¾ cup walnuts, chopped medium fine

Melt butter and white chocolate over simmering water in the top of a double boiler or in food-processor bowl—or in another small plastic or glass bowl—in a microwave oven at half power. When melted, whisk into a smooth, even mass. Measure instant espresso, extract, liqueur, crumbs, and nuts into the food-processor bowl; add the melted chocolate mixture; and process for 5-second intervals, checking texture frequently. It should be fine and dry, rather than mushy. Using walnut-sized nuggets of crust mix, press them no more than 1½ inches up the sides of a 10″ springform pan with your fingers. Wrapping your hand in plastic will give you better control and keep the mix from sticking to your fingers. Press and smooth down the remainder of the crust mix over the bottom of the springform pan with your fingers or the back of a soup spoon. If there are empty spaces in the bottom crust, press the sides a bit thinner and use the excess to fill in the blanks in the bottom, or just sprinkle some more cookie crumbs in the holes. Put the pan in the refrigerator to allow the crust to harden and set.

FILLING

3 ounces white chocolate

3 ounces dark chocolate

1 pound (2 8-ounce packages) cream cheese,
   each package cut into 8 squares

1 14-ounce can sweetened condensed milk

4 teaspoons Fruit Fresh

⅓ cup frozen orange juice concentrate, undiluted

1 tablespoon instant espresso

2 tablespoons coffee extract

1 ounce mocha-flavored chocolate bar,
    chopped or cut into chips

Melt white chocolate and dark chocolate separately over simmering water in the top of a double boiler, or in plastic bowls in a microwave oven on half power, and reserve. In a mixer or food processor, whip cream cheese, condensed milk and melted white chocolate until creamy and well blended. Dissolve Fruit Fresh in juice, add along with espresso and coffee extract to batter, and process until well combined. Reserve one cup batter. Fold mocha-flavored chips into the remaining batter and pour into crust, spreading the filling around carefully with a rubber spatula so that it's level and adheres to the sides of the crust. Add melted dark chocolate to reserved batter, pour into center of cake, and swirl with a knife to achieve a marble effect.

GARNISH

mocha-flavored chocolate bar, cut into chips,
    or chopped walnuts

Sprinkle cake with chopped mocha-flavored chocolate or walnuts. Place in the refrigerator to set until ready to serve.

Before serving, let cheesecake stand at room temperature for 10–15 minutes to allow the butter in the crust to loosen its bond with the metal ring. When you release the springform clasp, the crust will generally detach naturally from the sides. If it sticks, separate crust from the pan by inserting a metal spatula or sharp knife.

Nonbaked Piña Colada Cheesecake

CRUST

3 tablespoons butter

3 ounces white chocolate

½ cup finely ground vanilla-wafer crumbs

½ cup blanched almonds, chopped medium fine

¾ cup coconut flakes

Melt butter and white chocolate over simmering water in the top of a double boiler or in food-processor bowl—or another small plastic or glass bowl—in a microwave oven at half power. When melted, whisk into a smooth, even mass. Measure crumbs, nuts, and coconut flakes into the food-processor bowl; add the melted chocolate mixture; and process for 5-second intervals, checking texture frequently. It should be fine and dry, rather than mushy. Using walnut-sized nuggets of crust mix, press them no more than 1½ inches up the sides of a 10″ springform pan with your fingers. Wrapping your hand in plastic will give you better control and keep the mix from sticking to your fingers. Press and smooth down the remainder of the crust mix over the bottom of the springform pan with your fingers or the back of a soup spoon. If there are empty spaces in the bottom crust, press the sides a bit thinner and use the excess to fill in the blanks in the bottom, or just sprinkle some more cookie crumbs in the holes. Put the pan in the refrigerator to allow the crust to harden and set.

FILLING

2 dried pineapple rounds

2 tablespoons dark rum

3 ounces white chocolate

1 pound (2 8-ounce packages) cream cheese, each package cut into 8 squares

1 14-ounce can sweetened condensed milk

2 teaspoons Fruit Fresh

⅓ cup frozen pineapple juice concentrate, undiluted

2 tablespoons lime juice
1 teaspoon coconut extract
¼ cup coconut flakes

Cut the pineapple rounds into very thin slivers, soak in rum, and reserve. Melt white chocolate over simmering water in the top of a double boiler or in a plastic bowl in a microwave oven at half power, and reserve. In a mixer or food processor, whip cream cheese and condensed milk together until creamy and well blended. Dissolve Fruit Fresh in juices and extract, add to batter along with melted chocolate and process until well combined. Fold in slivered pineapple and coconut flakes. Pour into crust. Spread the filling around carefully with a rubber spatula so that it's level and adheres to the sides of the crust.

GARNISH
⅓ cup coconut flakes, lightly toasted in oven

Sprinkle cake with coconut and place in the refrigerator to set until ready to serve.

Before serving, let cheesecake stand at room temperature for 10–15 minutes to allow the butter in the crust to loosen its bond with the metal ring. When you release the springform clasp, the crust will generally detach naturally from the sides. If it sticks, separate crust from the pan by inserting a metal spatula or sharp knife.

Nonbaked Caribbean Banana Cheesecake

CRUST

3 tablespoons butter

5 ounces white chocolate

½ teaspoon banana flavoring

¾ cup finely ground vanilla-wafer crumbs

¼ cup dried banana chips, chopped medium fine

½ cup pecans, chopped medium fine

Melt butter and white chocolate over simmering water in the top of a double boiler or in food-processor bowl—or in another small plastic or glass bowl—in a microwave oven at half power. When melted, whisk into a smooth, even mass. Measure flavoring, crumbs, banana chips, and nuts into the food-processor bowl; add the melted chocolate mixture; and process for 5-second intervals, checking texture frequently. It should be fine and dry, rather than mushy. Using walnut-sized nuggets of crust mix, press them no more than 1½ inches up the sides of a 10″ springform pan with your fingers. Wrapping your hand in plastic will give you better control and keep the mix from sticking to your fingers. Press and smooth down the remainder of the crust mix over the bottom of the springform pan with your fingers or the back of a soup spoon. If there are empty spaces in the bottom crust, press the sides a bit thinner and use the excess to fill in the blanks in the bottom, or just sprinkle some more cookie crumbs in the holes. Put the pan in the refrigerator to allow the crust to harden and set.

FILLING

3 ounces white chocolate

1 pound (2 8-ounce packages) cream cheese, each package cut into 8 squares

1 14-ounce can sweetened condensed milk

4 teaspoons Fruit Fresh

⅓ cup frozen pineapple-orange-banana juice
    concentrate, undiluted
2   tablespoons lime juice
2   tablespoons lemon juice
1   teaspoon banana flavoring
2   teaspoons dark rum
1½ very ripe bananas, mashed
½   ripe banana, sliced thin

Melt white chocolate over simmering water in the top of a double boiler or in a plastic bowl in a microwave oven at half power, and reserve. In a mixer or food processor, whip cream cheese and condensed milk together until creamy and well blended. Dissolve Fruit Fresh in juices. Add to the batter with reserved chocolate, flavoring, rum, and mashed bananas, and process until well combined. Fold in sliced bananas and pour into crust. Spread the filling around carefully with a rubber spatula so that it's level and adheres to the sides of the crust.

GARNISH
12 whole banana chips

Insert banana chips so they stick up out of the batter in a clock pattern and place cake in the refrigerator to set until ready to serve.

Before serving, let cheesecake stand at room temperature for 10–15 minutes to allow the butter in the crust to loosen its bond with the metal ring. When you release the springform clasp, the crust will generally detach naturally from the sides. If it sticks, separate crust from the pan by inserting a metal spatula or sharp knife.

Nonbaked Butter Rum Cordial Cheesecake

CRUST

3 tablespoons butter

5 ounces butterscotch bits

1 teaspoon dark rum

¾ cup finely ground vanilla-wafer crumbs

¾ cup blanched almonds, chopped medium fine

Melt butter and butterscotch bits over simmering water in the top of a double boiler or in food-processor bowl—or in another small plastic or glass bowl—in a microwave oven at half power. When melted, whisk into a smooth, even mass. Measure rum, crumbs, and nuts into the food-processor bowl; add the melted butterscotch mixture; and process for 5-second intervals, checking texture frequently. It should be fine and dry, rather than mushy. Using walnut-sized nuggets of crust mix, press them no more than 1½ inches up the sides of a 10″ springform pan with your fingers. Wrapping your hand in plastic will give you better control and keep the mix from sticking to your fingers. Press and smooth down the remainder of the crust mix over the bottom of the springform pan with your fingers or the back of a soup spoon. If there are empty spaces in the bottom crust, press the sides a bit thinner and use the excess to fill in the blanks in the bottom, or just sprinkle some more cookie crumbs in the holes. Put the pan in the refrigerator to allow the crust to harden and set.

FILLING

5 ounces butterscotch bits

1 pound (2 8-ounce packages) cream cheese,
    each package cut into 8 squares

1 14-ounce can sweetened condensed milk

4 teaspoons Fruit Fresh

¼ cup dark rum

2 tablespoons lemon juice

2 tablespoons lime juice
¼ cup chopped almonds
⅓ cup chocolate-covered rum cordials

Melt butterscotch bits over simmering water in the top of a double boiler, or in a microwave oven on half power, and reserve. In a mixer or food processor, whip cream cheese and condensed milk until creamy and well blended. Dissolve Fruit Fresh in rum and juices, and add along with melted butterscotch bits and almonds to processor bowl and process until well combined. Pour into crust. Spread the filling around carefully with a rubber spatula so that it's level and adheres to the sides of the crust. Insert the rum cordials into the batter so they do not show and will be a surprise taste treat.

GARNISH
1 ounce butterscotch bits, melted

Drizzle melted butterscotch bits on top of cake. Place in the refrigerator to set until ready to serve.

Before serving, let cheesecake stand at room temperature for 10–15 minutes to allow the butter in the crust to loosen its bond with the metal ring. When you release the springform clasp, the crust will generally detach naturally from the sides. If it sticks, separate crust from the pan by inserting a metal spatula or sharp knife.

Nonbaked Butter Brandy Brickle Cheesecake

CRUST

3   tablespoons butter

3   ounces white chocolate

1   teaspoon brandy

¾   cup finely ground shortbread-cookie crumbs

¾   cup cashews or walnuts, chopped medium
      fine

Melt butter and white chocolate over simmering water in the top of a double boiler or in food-processor bowl—or in another small plastic or glass bowl—in a microwave oven at half power. When melted, whisk into a smooth, even mass. Measure brandy, crumbs, and nuts into the food-processor bowl; add the melted chocolate mixture; and process for 5-second intervals, checking texture frequently. It should be fine and dry, rather than mushy. Using walnut-sized nuggets of crust mix, press them no more than 1½ inches up the sides of a 10″ springform pan with your fingers. Wrapping your hand in plastic will give you better control and keep the mix from sticking to your fingers. Press and smooth down the remainder of the crust mix over the bottom of the springform pan with your fingers or the back of a soup spoon. If there are empty spaces in the bottom crust, press the sides a bit thinner and use the excess to fill in the blanks in the bottom, or just sprinkle some more cookie crumbs in the holes. Put the pan in the refrigerator to allow the crust to harden and set.

FILLING

3   ounces white chocolate

2   ounces butterscotch bits

1   pound (2 8-ounce packages) cream cheese,
      each package cut into 8 squares

1   14-ounce can sweetened condensed milk

½   teaspoon butterscotch extract

2   teaspoons brandy extract

2   tablespoons brandy

2   ounces chocolate almond crunch, chopped or
       diced

Melt white chocolate and butterscotch bits together over simmering water in the top of a double boiler, in food-processor bowls, or another plastic bowl, in a microwave oven at half power. In a mixer or food processor, whip cream cheese, condensed milk, melted chocolate and butterscotch bits, extracts, and brandy together until creamy and well blended. Fold in chopped almond crunch. Pour into crust. Spread the filling around carefully with a rubber spatula so that it's level and adheres to the sides of the crust.

GARNISH

Chocolate almond crunch, chopped

Sprinkle crunch on top of cake and put into refrigerator to set.

Before serving, let cheesecake stand at room temperature for 10–15 minutes to allow the butter in the crust to loosen its bond with the metal ring. When you release the springform clasp, the crust will generally detach naturally from the sides. If it sticks, separate crust from the pan by inserting a metal spatula or sharp knife.

Nonbaked Caramel Nut Cheesecake

CRUST

3 tablespoons butter

3 ounces white chocolate

¾ teaspoon caramel flavoring

¾ cup finely ground vanilla-wafer crumbs

¾ cup pecans, chopped medium fine

Melt butter and white chocolate over simmering water in the top of a double boiler or in food-processor bowl—or in another small plastic or glass bowl—in a microwave oven at half power. When melted, whisk into a smooth, even mass. Measure caramel flavoring, crumbs, and nuts into the food-processor bowl; add the melted chocolate mixture; and process for 5-second intervals, checking texture frequently. It should be fine and dry, rather than mushy. Using walnut-sized nuggets of crust mix, press them no more than 1½ inches up the sides of a 10″ springform pan with your fingers. Wrapping your hand in plastic will give you better control and keep the mix from sticking to your fingers. Press and smooth down the remainder of the crust mix over the bottom of the springform pan with your fingers or the back of a soup spoon. If there are empty spaces in the bottom crust, press the sides a bit thinner and use the excess to fill in the blanks in the bottom, or just sprinkle some more cookie crumbs in the holes. Put the pan in the refrigerator to allow the crust to harden and set.

FILLING

5 ounces white chocolate

1 pound (2 8-ounce packages) cream cheese,
   each package cut into 8 squares

1 14-ounce can sweetened condensed milk

2 teaspoons Fruit Fresh

3 tablespoons lemon juice

1 teaspoon caramel flavoring

Melt white chocolate over simmering water in the top of a double boiler or in a microwave oven at half power, and reserve. In a mixer or food processor, whip cream cheese and condensed milk together until creamy and well blended. Dissolve Fruit Fresh in lemon juice and add along with caramel flavoring and melted chocolate to processor bowl and process until well combined. Pour into crust. Spread the filling around carefully with a rubber spatula so that it's level and adheres to the sides of the crust.

GARNISH

½ cup chopped pecans
¼ cup caramel-flavored topping, warmed

Sprinkle pecans on cake. Drizzle topping around them and swirl with the point of a knife to make an attractive pattern. Put in refrigerator to set.

Before serving, let cheesecake stand at room temperature for 10–15 minutes to allow the butter in the crust to loosen its bond with the metal ring. When you release the springform clasp, the crust will generally detach naturally from the sides. If it sticks, separate crust from the pan by inserting a metal spatula or sharp knife.

Nonbaked Tropical Fruit Cheesecake

CRUST

  3 tablespoons butter

  3 ounces white chocolate

  1 teaspoon coconut extract

  ¾ cup finely ground vanilla-wafer crumbs

  6 tablespoons almonds, chopped medium fine

  2 tablespoons coconut flakes

  1½ ounces dried papaya, cut into ½-inch dice

Melt butter and white chocolate over simmering water in the top of a double boiler or in food-processor bowl—or in another small plastic or glass bowl—in a microwave oven at half power. When melted, whisk into a smooth, even mass. Measure extract, crumbs, nuts, coconut, and papaya into the food-processor bowl; add the melted chocolate mixture; and process for 5-second intervals, checking texture frequently. It should be fine and dry, rather than mushy. Using walnut-sized nuggets of crust mix, press them no more than 1½ inches up the sides of a 10″ springform pan with your fingers. Wrapping your hand in plastic will give you better control and keep the mix from sticking to your fingers. Press and smooth down the remainder of the crust mix over the bottom of the springform pan with your fingers or the back of a soup spoon. If there are empty spaces in the bottom crust, press the sides a bit thinner and use the excess to fill in the blanks in the bottom, or just sprinkle some more cookie crumbs in the holes. Put the pan in the refrigerator to allow the crust to harden and set.

FILLING

  1 ounce dried papaya

  1 tablespoon light rum

  3 ounces white chocolate

  1 pound (2 8-ounce packages) cream cheese,
      each package cut into 8 squares

  1 14-ounce can sweetened condensed milk

  4 teaspoons Fruit Fresh

2 tablespoons lime juice

2 tablespoons lemon juice

⅓ cup frozen tropical juice concentrate, undiluted

Slice dried papaya very thinly, soak in rum, and reserve. Melt white chocolate over simmering water in the top of a double boiler, or in a microwave oven at half power, and reserve. In a mixer or food processor, whip cream cheese and condensed milk together until creamy and well blended. Dissolve Fruit Fresh in juices and add to processor bowl along with melted chocolate, and process until well combined. Fold in papaya and rum. Pour into crust. Spread the filling around carefully with a rubber spatula so that it's level and adheres to the sides of the crust.

GARNISH

⅓ cup coconut flakes, lightly toasted

Sprinkle cake with coconut flakes and place in refrigerator to set.

Before serving, let cheesecake stand at room temperature for 10–15 minutes to allow the butter in the crust to loosen its bond with the metal ring. When you release the springform clasp, the crust will generally detach naturally from the sides. If it sticks, separate crust from the pan by inserting a metal spatula or sharp knife.

Nonbaked Coco-Mango Cheesecake

CRUST

3 tablespoons butter

5 ounces white chocolate

1 teaspoon coconut extract

¾ cup finely ground vanilla-wafer crumbs

¾ cup macadamia nuts, chopped medium fine

Melt butter and white chocolate over simmering water in the top of a double boiler or in food-processor bowl—or in another small plastic or glass bowl—in a microwave oven at half power. When melted, whisk into a smooth, even mass. Measure extract, crumbs, and nuts into the food-processor bowl; add the melted chocolate mixture; and process for 5-second intervals, checking texture frequently. It should be fine and dry, rather than mushy. Using walnut-sized nuggets of crust mix, press them no more than 1½ inches up the sides of a 10″ springform pan with your fingers. Wrapping your hand in plastic will give you better control and keep the mix from sticking to your fingers. Press and smooth down the remainder of the crust mix over the bottom of the springform pan with your fingers or the back of a soup spoon. If there are empty spaces in the bottom crust, press the sides a bit thinner and use the excess to fill in the blanks in the bottom, or just sprinkle some more cookie crumbs in the holes. Put the pan in the refrigerator to allow the crust to harden and set.

FILLING

4 ounces white chocolate

1 pound (2 8-ounce packages) cream cheese,
     each package cut into 8 squares

1 14-ounce can sweetened condensed milk

2 tablespoons Fruit Fresh

⅓ cup frozen pineapple-orange juice
     concentrate, undiluted

2 tablespoons mango or pineapple extract

1 tablespoon anisette liqueur

1 cup chopped fresh ripe mango

Melt white chocolate over simmering water in the top of a double boiler or in a plastic bowl in a microwave oven at half power, and reserve. In a mixer or food processor, whip cream cheese and condensed milk together until creamy and well blended. Dissolve Fruit Fresh in juice, extract, and anisette, add to processor bowl along with melted chocolate, and process until well combined. Fold in mango. Pour into crust. Spread the filling around carefully with a rubber spatula so that it's level and adheres to the sides of the crust.

GARNISH

⅓ cup coconut flakes, lightly toasted in oven

Sprinkle cake with coconut flakes and place in the refrigerator to set.

Before serving, let cheesecake stand at room temperature for 10–15 minutes to allow the butter in the crust to loosen its bond with the metal ring. When you release the springform clasp, the crust will generally detach naturally from the sides. If it sticks, separate crust from the pan by inserting a metal spatula or sharp knife.

Nonbaked Banana-Split Cheesecake

CRUST

3 tablespoons butter

3 ounces sweet or semisweet chocolate

½ cup finely ground chocolate-wafer crumbs

¼ cup finely ground vanilla-wafer crumbs

¾ cup walnuts, chopped medium fine

Melt butter and chocolate over simmering water in the top of a double boiler or in food-processor bowl—or in another small plastic or glass bowl—in a microwave oven at half power. When melted, whisk into a smooth, even mass. Measure crumbs and nuts into the food-processor bowl, add the melted chocolate mixture, and process for 5-second intervals, checking texture frequently. It should be fine and dry, rather than mushy. Using walnut-sized nuggets of crust mix, press them no more than 1½ inches up the sides of a 10″ springform pan with your fingers. Wrapping your hand in plastic will give you better control and keep the mix from sticking to your fingers. Press and smooth down the remainder of the crust mix over the bottom of the springform pan with your fingers or the back of a soup spoon. If there are empty spaces in the bottom crust, press the sides a bit thinner and use the excess to fill in the blanks in the bottom, or just sprinkle some more cookie crumbs in the holes. Put the pan in the refrigerator to allow the crust to harden and set.

FILLING

2 ounces sweet or semisweet chocolate

1 pound (2 8-ounce packages) cream cheese,
      each package cut into 8 squares

1 14-ounce can sweetened condensed milk

4 teaspoons Fruit Fresh

⅓ cup frozen pineapple-orange-banana juice
      concentrate, undiluted

2 tablespoons lime juice

2 tablespoons lemon juice

½ teaspoon banana flavoring

1 very ripe banana, mashed

1 ripe banana, sliced thin

¼ cup "wet" nuts, from walnut dessert topping,
   drained and chopped

Melt chocolate over simmering water in the top of a double boiler or in a plastic bowl in a microwave oven at half power, and reserve. In a mixer or food processor, whip cream cheese and condensed milk together until creamy and well blended. Remove one cup of batter, add chocolate to it, and reserve. Dissolve Fruit Fresh in juices, add with flavoring and mashed banana to batter in processor bowl, and process until well combined. Fold in sliced banana and nuts and pour into crust. Spread the filling around carefully with a rubber spatula so that it's level and adheres to the sides of the crust. Add reserved chocolate batter to middle and cut through several times with a knife to achieve a marbled effect. Place in refrigerator to set until ready to serve.

Before serving, let cheesecake stand at room temperature for 10–15 minutes to allow the butter in the crust to loosen its bond with the metal ring. When you release the springform clasp, the crust will generally detach naturally from the sides. If it sticks, separate crust from the pan by inserting a metal spatula or sharp knife. Slice and garnish.

GARNISH

hot fudge sauce, warmed

whipped cream

maraschino cherries

Drizzle a spoonful of hot fudge sauce on each slice. Top with a dollop of whipped cream and one maraschino cherry, just like a banana split.

Nonbaked Mandarin Orange Cheesecake

CRUST

3 tablespoons butter

5 ounces white chocolate

2 teaspoons Grand Marnier

¾ cup finely ground shortbread-cookie crumbs

¾ cup blanched almonds, chopped medium fine

Melt butter and white chocolate over simmering water in the top of a double boiler or in food-processor bowl—or in another small plastic or glass bowl—in a microwave oven at half power. When melted, whisk into a smooth, even mass. Measure Grand Marnier, crumbs, and nuts into the food-processor bowl; add the melted chocolate mixture; and process for 5-second intervals, checking texture frequently. It should be fine and dry, rather than mushy. Using walnut-sized nuggets of crust mix, press them no more than 1½ inches up the sides of a 10″ springform pan with your fingers. Wrapping your hand in plastic will give you better control and keep the mix from sticking to your fingers. Press and smooth down the remainder of the crust mix over the bottom of the springform pan with your fingers or the back of a soup spoon. If there are empty spaces in the bottom crust, press the sides a bit thinner and use the excess to fill in the blanks in the bottom, or just sprinkle some more cookie crumbs in the holes. Put the pan in the refrigerator to allow the crust to harden and set.

FILLING

5 ounces white chocolate

1 pound (2 8-ounce packages) cream cheese,
   each package cut into 8 squares

1 14-ounce can sweetened condensed milk

4 teaspoons Fruit Fresh

⅓ cup frozen orange juice concentrate, undiluted

2 tablespoons lemon juice

1 teaspoon Grand Marnier

1 teaspoon orange extract

¾ teaspoon almond extract

1 14-ounce can mandarin orange segments,
    drained and blotted

Melt white chocolate over simmering water in the top of a double boiler or in a plastic bowl in a microwave oven at half power, and reserve. In a mixer or food processor, whip cream cheese and condensed milk together until creamy and well blended. Dissolve Fruit Fresh into juices, and add along with Grand Marnier, extracts, and melted chocolate to the food-processor bowl and blend until well combined. Reserve 12 orange segments for garnish and fold the rest into the batter with a rubber spatula. Pour into crust and spread the filling around carefully with a rubber spatula so that it's level and adheres to the sides of the crust.

GARNISH

12 reserved mandarin orange segments

Place orange segments around the rim of the cake like the numbers on a clock face. Place in the refrigerator to set until ready to serve.

Before serving, let cheesecake stand at room temperature for 10–15 minutes to allow the butter in the crust to loosen its bond with the metal ring. When you release the springform clasp, the crust will generally detach naturally from the sides. If it sticks, separate crust from the pan by inserting a metal spatula or sharp knife.

Nonbaked Framboise Cheesecake

CRUST

3 tablespoons butter

4 ounces white chocolate

1 teaspoon raspberry extract

¾ cup finely ground vanilla-wafer crumbs

¾ cup pine nuts, chopped medium fine

Melt butter and white chocolate over simmering water in the top of a double boiler or in food-processor bowl—or in another small plastic or glass bowl—in a microwave oven at half power. When melted, whisk into a smooth, even mass. Measure extract, crumbs, and nuts into the food-processor bowl; add the melted chocolate mixture; and process for 5-second intervals, checking texture frequently. It should be fine and dry, rather than mushy. Using walnut-sized nuggets of crust mix, press them no more than 1½ inches up the sides of a 10″ springform pan with your fingers. Wrapping your hand in plastic will give you better control and keep the mix from sticking to your fingers. Press and smooth down the remainder of the crust mix over the bottom of the springform pan with your fingers or the back of a soup spoon. If there are empty spaces in the bottom crust, press the sides a bit thinner and use the excess to fill in the blanks in the bottom, or just sprinkle some more cookie crumbs in the holes. Put the pan in the refrigerator to allow the crust to harden and set.

FILLING

5 ounces white chocolate

1 pound (2 8-ounce packages) cream cheese, each package cut into 8 squares

1 14-ounce can sweetened condensed milk

2 teaspoons Fruit Fresh

3 tablespoons lemon juice

1 tablespoon Framboise or raspberry liqueur

1 cup fresh or frozen raspberries

Melt white chocolate over simmering water in the top of a double boiler or in a plastic bowl in a microwave oven at half power, and reserve. In a mixer or food processor, whip cream cheese and condensed milk together until creamy and well blended. Dissolve Fruit Fresh in juice and add to batter in processor bowl along with liqueur and melted chocolate, and process until well combined. Fold in raspberries with a rubber spatula, taking care not to mash them. Pour into crust. Spread the filling around carefully with a rubber spatula so that it's level and adheres to the sides of the crust.

GARNISH
1 ounce white chocolate, melted
1 cup fresh raspberries

Drizzle white chocolate on top of the cake, and place raspberries in an attractive pattern around it. Place in the refrigerator to set until ready to serve.

Before serving, let cheesecake stand at room temperature for 10–15 minutes to allow the butter in the crust to loosen its bond with the metal ring. When you release the springform clasp, the crust will generally detach naturally from the sides. If it sticks, separate crust from the pan by inserting a metal spatula or sharp knife.

Nonbaked Raspberry Rhubarb Cheesecake

PRELIMINARY

1 pound frozen rhubarb

¼ cup water

¾ cup sugar

Boil rhubarb and water together for 5 minutes, then add sugar and simmer, covered, for 20 minutes more. Use this time to make the crust and prepare the batter. When rhubarb is cooked, drain and discard juices and reserve rhubarb pieces.

CRUST

3 tablespoons butter

3 ounces white chocolate

1 teaspoon raspberry extract

¾ cup finely ground tea-biscuit crumbs

¾ cup pine nuts, chopped medium fine

Melt butter and white chocolate over simmering water in the top of a double boiler or in food-processor bowl—or in another small plastic or glass bowl—in a microwave oven at half power. When melted, whisk into a smooth, even mass. Measure extract, crumbs, and nuts into the food-processor bowl; add the melted chocolate mixture; and process for 5-second intervals, checking texture frequently. It should be fine and dry, rather than mushy. Using walnut-sized nuggets of crust mix, press them no more than 1½ inches up the sides of a 10″ springform pan with your fingers. Wrapping your hand in plastic will give you better control and keep the mix from sticking to your fingers. Press and smooth down the remainder of the crust mix over the bottom of the springform pan with your fingers or the back of a soup spoon. If there are empty spaces in the bottom crust, press the sides a bit thinner and use the excess to fill in the blanks in the bottom, or just sprinkle some more cookie crumbs in the holes. Put the pan in the refrigerator to allow the crust to harden and set.

FILLING

5 ounces white chocolate

1 pound (2 8-ounce packages) cream cheese,
   each package cut into 8 squares

1 14-ounce can sweetened condensed milk

4 teaspoons Fruit Fresh

3 tablespoons lemon juice

1 tablespoon Framboise or raspberry liqueur
   reserved cooked rhubarb

Melt white chocolate over simmering water in the top of a double boiler or in a plastic bowl in a microwave oven at half power, and reserve. In a mixer or food processor, whip cream cheese and condensed milk together until creamy and well blended. Dissolve Fruit Fresh in lemon juice, add with raspberry liqueur and melted white chocolate to the batter, and blend until well combined. Fold in cooked rhubarb and pour into crust. Spread the filling around carefully with a rubber spatula so that it's level and adheres to the sides of the crust.

GARNISH

½ cup fresh or frozen defrosted raspberries

½ cup coconut flakes

Decorate top of cake with raspberries and sprinkle with coconut flakes. Place in the refrigerator to set until ready to serve.

Before serving, let cheesecake stand at room temperature for 10–15 minutes to allow the butter in the crust to loosen its bond with the metal ring. When you release the springform clasp, the crust will generally detach naturally from the sides. If it sticks, separate crust from the pan by inserting a metal spatula or sharp knife.

Nonbaked Cran-Cherry Cheesecake

CRUST

3 tablespoons butter

4 ounces white chocolate

¾ cup finely ground vanilla-wafer crumbs

¾ cup blanched almonds, chopped medium fine

Melt butter and white chocolate over simmering water in the top of a double boiler or in food-processor bowl—or in another small plastic or glass bowl—in a microwave oven at half power. When melted, whisk into a smooth, even mass. Measure crumbs and nuts into the food-processor bowl, add the melted chocolate mixture, and process for 5-second intervals, checking texture frequently. It should be fine and dry, rather than mushy. Using walnut-sized nuggets of crust mix, press them no more than 1½ inches up the sides of a 10″ springform pan with your fingers. Wrapping your hand in plastic will give you better control and keep the mix from sticking to your fingers. Press and smooth down the remainder of the crust mix over the bottom of the springform pan with your fingers or the back of a soup spoon. If there are empty spaces in the bottom crust, press the sides a bit thinner and use the excess to fill in the blanks in the bottom, or just sprinkle some more cookie crumbs in the holes. Put the pan in the refrigerator to allow the crust to harden and set.

FILLING

5 ounces white chocolate

1 pound (2 8-ounce packages) cream cheese, each package cut into 8 squares

1 14-ounce can sweetened condensed milk

2 tablespoons Fruit Fresh

3 tablespoons lemon juice

1 tablespoon cranberry juice concentrate, bottled or frozen and undiluted

1 teaspoon cranberry extract

1½ cups tart, pitted canned cherries, drained

Melt white chocolate over simmering water in the top of a double boiler or in a plastic bowl in a microwave oven at half power, and reserve. In a mixer or food processor, whip cream cheese and condensed milk together until creamy and well blended. Dissolve Fruit Fresh in juices and add with melted chocolate and cranberry extract to the batter and process until well combined. Fold in cherries with a rubber spatula. Pour into crust. Spread the filling around carefully with a rubber spatula so that it's level and adheres to the sides of the crust.

GARNISH
1 cup canned cherries, drained

Place cherries on the top of the cake in an attractive pattern, and place in the refrigerator to set until ready to serve.

Before serving, let cheesecake stand at room temperature for 10–15 minutes to allow the butter in the crust to loosen its bond with the metal ring. When you release the springform clasp, the crust will generally detach naturally from the sides. If it sticks, separate crust from the pan by inserting a metal spatula or sharp knife.

Nonbaked Holiday Ginger Pumpkin Cheesecake

CRUST

3   tablespoons butter

4   ounces white chocolate

1   teaspoon brandy

¾   cup finely ground gingersnap or spiced-wafer
      crumbs

¾   cup walnuts, chopped medium fine

Melt butter and white chocolate over simmering water in the top of a double boiler or in food-processor bowl—or in another small plastic or glass bowl—in a microwave oven at half power. When melted, whisk into a smooth, even mass. Measure brandy, crumbs, and nuts into the food-processor bowl; add the melted chocolate mixture; and process for 5-second intervals, checking texture frequently. It should be fine and dry, rather than mushy. Using walnut-sized nuggets of crust mix, press them no more than 1½ inches up the sides of a 10″ springform pan with your fingers. Wrapping your hand in plastic will give you better control and keep the mix from sticking to your fingers. Press and smooth down the remainder of the crust mix over the bottom of the springform pan with your fingers or the back of a soup spoon. If there are empty spaces in the bottom crust, press the sides a bit thinner and use the excess to fill in the blanks in the bottom, or just sprinkle some more cookie crumbs in the holes. Put the pan in the refrigerator to allow the crust to harden and set.

FILLING

5   ounces white chocolate

1   pound (2 8-ounce packages) cream cheese,
      each package cut into 8 squares

1   14-ounce can sweetened condensed milk

1   cup canned pumpkin

        2 teaspoons Fruit Fresh
      ⅓ cup frozen orange juice concentrate, undiluted
        2 tablespoons lemon juice
        1 teaspoon brandy or brandy extract
      ¾ teaspoon ground cinnamon
      ⅛ teaspoon ground mace
           pinch of ground nutmeg
        2 tablespoons maple syrup
      ¼ cup chopped walnuts
        1 ounce crystallized ginger, thinly sliced or finely
           diced

Melt white chocolate over simmering water in the top of a double boiler or in a plastic bowl in a microwave oven at half power, and reserve. In a mixer or food processor, whip cream cheese, condensed milk, and pumpkin together until creamy and well blended. Dissolve Fruit Fresh into juices and add with brandy, melted white chocolate, cinnamon, mace, nutmeg, maple syrup, and chopped walnuts to batter, and process until well combined. Fold in ginger with a rubber spatula and pour into crust. Spread the filling around carefully with a rubber spatula so that it's level and adheres to the sides of the crust.

GARNISH
        2 ounces crystallized ginger, thinly sliced

Place ginger slices around the top of the cheesecake like the numbers on a clock face and place in the refrigerator to set until ready to serve.

Before serving, let cheesecake stand at room temperature for 10–15 minutes to allow the butter in the crust to loosen its bond with the metal ring. When you release the springform clasp, the crust will generally detach naturally from the sides. If it sticks, separate crust from the pan by inserting a metal spatula or sharp knife.

(cont'd)

**TOPPING FOR AN ESPECIALLY
FESTIVE APPEARANCE**

½ cup heavy cream

1 tablespoon confectioners' sugar

1 teaspoon brandy

   crystallized ginger, finely chopped

About an hour before serving, whip up cream, sugar, and brandy; put in a pastry bag that's fitted with a star tube; and pipe whipped-cream rosettes on top of cake. Sprinkle with ginger and keep cake refrigerated until ready to cut and serve.

Nonbaked Amaretto Cheesecake

CRUST

3 tablespoons butter

4 ounces white chocolate

1 teaspoon almond extract

¾ cup finely ground Italian amaretto-flavored
  biscotti crumbs

¾ cup slivered almonds with skin on them,
  chopped medium fine

Melt butter and white chocolate over simmering water in the top of a double boiler or in food-processor bowl—or in another small plastic or glass bowl—in a microwave oven at half power. When melted, whisk into a smooth, even mass. Measure extract, crumbs, and nuts into the food-processor bowl; add the melted chocolate mixture; and process for 5-second intervals, checking texture frequently. It should be fine and dry, rather than mushy. Using walnut-sized nuggets of crust mix, press them no more than 1½ inches up the sides of a 10″ springform pan with your fingers. Wrapping your hand in plastic will give you better control and keep the mix from sticking to your fingers. Press and smooth down the remainder of the crust mix over the bottom of the springform pan with your fingers or the back of a soup spoon. If there are empty spaces in the bottom crust, press the sides a bit thinner and use the excess to fill in the blanks in the bottom, or just sprinkle some more cookie crumbs in the holes. Put the pan in the refrigerator to allow the crust to harden and set.

FILLING

5 ounces white chocolate

1 pound (2 8-ounce packages) cream cheese,
  each package cut into 8 squares

1 14-ounce can sweetened condensed milk

3 teaspoons Fruit Fresh

2 tablespoons lemon juice

1 tablespoon amaretto liqueur

1 teaspoon almond extract

1 cup slivered almonds with skin on them

Melt white chocolate over simmering water in the top of a double boiler or in a plastic bowl in a microwave oven at half power, and reserve. In a mixer or food processor, whip cream cheese and condensed milk together until creamy and well blended. Dissolve Fruit Fresh in lemon juice and add with liqueur, extract, and melted chocolate to the batter, and blend until well combined. Fold in slivered almonds and pour into crust. Spread the filling around carefully with a rubber spatula so that it's level and adheres to the sides of the crust.

GARNISH

½ cup slivered almonds with skin on them

Sprinkle cake with almonds and place in the refrigerator to set until ready to serve.

Before serving, let cheesecake stand at room temperature for 10–15 minutes to allow the butter in the crust to loosen its bond with the metal ring. When you release the springform clasp, the crust will generally detach naturally from the sides. If it sticks, separate crust from the pan by inserting a metal spatula or sharp knife.

BONUS!

The Magic Formula Which Will Allow
You to Experiment and Concoct Your Own
Personally Flavored Nonbaked Cheesecakes

CRUST

3 tablespoons butter

4 ounces chocolate or flavored chips like
    butterscotch, peanut butter, etc.

1 teaspoon flavored extract (optional)

¾ cup finely ground cookie crumbs

¾ cup nuts, chopped medium fine

Melt butter and chocolate or flavored chips over simmering water in the top of a double boiler or in food-processor bowl, or another plastic bowl in a microwave oven at half power. When melted, whisk into a smooth, even mass. Measure optional extract, crumbs, and nuts into the food-processor bowl; add the melted chocolate-butter mixture; and process for 5-second intervals, checking texture frequently. It should be fine and dry, rather than mushy. Using walnut-sized nuggets of crust mix, press them no more than 1½ inches up the sides of a 10″ springform pan with your fingers. Wrapping your hand in plastic will give you better control and keep the mix from sticking to your fingers. Press and smooth down the remainder of the crust mix over the bottom of the springform pan with your fingers or the back of a soup spoon. If there are empty spaces in the bottom crust, press the sides a bit thinner and use the excess to fill in the blanks in the bottom, or just sprinkle some more cookie crumbs in the holes. Put the pan in the refrigerator to allow the crust to harden and set.

FILLING

4–5 ounces of some kind of chocolate or flavored
    chips like butterscotch, peanut butter, etc.

1 pound (2 8-ounce packages) cream cheese,
    each package cut into 8 squares

1 14-ounce can sweetened condensed milk

⅓ cup lemon juice

2 teaspoons extract, flavoring, or liqueur

½ cup nut pieces, dried fruits, or fresh fruits
    cut into slivers

Melt chocolate or flavored chips over simmering water in the top of a double boiler or in a plastic bowl in a microwave oven at half power, and reserve. In a mixer or food processor, whip cream cheese, condensed milk, juice, extract, flavoring, or liqueur together until creamy and well blended. Fold in nuts or dried or fresh fruits and pour into crust. Spread the filling around carefully with a rubber spatula so that it's level and adheres to the sides of the crust.

GARNISH

chopped nuts or dried or fresh fruits, cut into
    slivers

Garnish cake and place in the refrigerator to set until ready to serve.

Before serving, let cheesecake stand at room temperature for 10–15 minutes to allow the butter in the crust to loosen its bond with the metal ring. When you release the springform clasp, the crust will generally detach naturally from the sides. If it sticks, separate crust from the pan by inserting a metal spatula or sharp knife.

CHIC CHEESECAKE MUFFINS

$\mathcal{M}$uffins are chic now, and where anything is chic, cheesecake rules. Cheesecake muffins (or call them cupcakes—we don't care) should come in creative, fun flavors. As you'll see from the following recipes, our imaginations have run wild.

Cheesecake muffins are perfect for children's parties. They travel well, so you can pack them in a lunch box or take them on a picnic. They also freeze nicely, defrost quickly, and can be ready to serve in a jiffy. And if you can't decide if your guests prefer chocolate, Irish cream, or raspberry? Not to worry. It's easy enough to make and offer your friends three or more varieties.

READ BEFORE MAKING!

The results of our investigation of muffin tins, pans, and cups indicate that there are variations in size and volume among several of those that are considered standard, which we've itemized on the following chart:

SIZE	NUMBER PER PAN	DEPTH	DIAMETER
Giant	6	1¼"	3¼"
Standard #1	12	1¼"	2¾"
Standard #2	12	1⅛"	1⅝"
Standard #3	6	1¼"	2¾"
Teensy	12	⅞"	1¾"

NOTE: Standard #3 is the same as the aluminum-foil discardable tins.

Three tablespoons of crust mix will line any standard muffin cup, and ¼ cup of batter should fill one satisfactorily. For tiny muffinettes, one tablespoon of crust mix and a heaping tablespoon of filling should suffice. We prefer to make muffinettes with nonbaked fillings. Baking the muffinettes requires more attention than most of us have to spare.

The following recipe proportions will make twelve muffins. If you want to make fewer, divide by two and just make six, or six of one kind and six of another.

Important Information About Nonbaked Cheesecake Muffins

Naturally, we prefer nonbaked cheesecake muffins because they're easier to make, and there's no waiting period while they bake and cool. Consequently, nine of the following ten cheesecake muffins are also nonbaked. They contain a small amount of batter, so they set quickly. They should set in the refrigerator, but if you're in a real hurry, put them directly into the freezer for 30–40 minutes, and they'll be edible. We try to freeze three from each batch of a dozen we make so we can serve assorted flavors later. Do this and your friends will marvel at your culinary legerdemain.

Nonbaked batter can be beaten in a mixer, but since each batch of filling (twelve muffins worth) contains only 8–11 ounces of cream cheese, using a food processor will provide you with a smoother, more uniform batter.

You may well ask what you should do if you have no food processor. The answer is simple:

GET ONE!

Lining each muffin-tin cup with a paper baking cup enhances a muffin's appearance. Naturally, we tried the fancy, expensive, imported cup liners first; but in the end, we prefer the foil-laminated baking cups ($2\frac{1}{2}$-inch diameter) that were for sale at the neighborhood supermarket. Some cup liners will be slightly wider than the muffin cups and may jut out of the tins initially, but the lining of crust will stabilize and solidify them. We prefer to make our nonbaked muffins in the aluminum throwaway tins because the baking cup liners fit those muffin cups best. We freeze our leftover nonbaked muffins in the throwaway tins as well because the tins stack in the freezer so nicely and can be used over and over without serious washing.

For nonbaked muffins, metal cups can also be lined with a 6-inch square of plastic wrap. Tiny muffinette cups should be lined only with plastic wrap. The overhang helps you lift out the set, chilled cheesecake muffin. Naturally, you'll strip off the plastic wrap before serving. If you press crust mix against a naked metal muffin cup, you may have to run a sharp knife around the sides to remove the finished muffin, but there's enough butter in the crust to keep it from sticking once the crust stands at room temperature for a few minutes.

If you're afraid your fingers are too klutzy to maneuver those crumbs around the baking cup or muffin tin, relax and remember the basic rule of crumb crusts: Press small amounts of the mix against the sides of the muffin cup first. Another helpful technique is to flatten a nugget of crust mix against the side of your mixing bowl and then transfer this flattened slab to the sides of your muffin cup. Wrapping your fingers in plastic wrap will help control a buttery crust.

Since our crust-mix proportions are generous, you may have leftovers. Never discard them! Instead, line additional cup liners with crust mix, chill them, stack them, wrap them in foil, and freeze them. If you have a small quantity only, make crusts for muffinettes. At some future date, when you have surplus batter, you can fill those perfectly good prefrozen crusts with it.

Leftover crust mix can also be frozen in a glob. Later, different batches can be zapped and warmed in the microwave, individually or together. Leftover crust mix can extend a skimpy crust. Suppose you have all the batter ingredients but are missing something for a crust. Zap all those leftover crust globs and, voilà! there's your crust.

Notice that we specify finely ground nuts for the nonbaked cheesecake muffin crust mix. The finer and mushier the crust blend, the more easily it sculpts into a cup.

Important Information About Baked Cheesecake Muffins

Baked cheesecake muffins can be prepared in foil or paper baking cups. Muffin cups can also be lined with a 6-inch-square sheet of aluminum foil. A third alternative is to lay a 1″ × 7″ strip of aluminum foil down the side, across the bottom, and up the other side of a muffin cup, like a stirrup. Press your crust into the cup, fill it with batter, bake, and chill. When the muffin is ready to serve, let it sit at room temperature for a few minutes, and then pull on both ends of the stirrup to lift the muffin out.

CHESSECAKE MUFFIN RECIPES

*Ginger Peachy Nonbaked
Cheesecake Muffins*

CRUST

5 tablespoons lightly salted butter

6 ounces white chocolate

1 cup finely ground gingersnap crumbs

1 cup finely ground pine nuts

Melt butter and chocolate together over simmering water in the top of a double boiler, or in a microwave oven at half power, and reserve. Blend crumbs and nuts together in a food processor and then add chocolate mixture and pulse until well combined. Line the cups of a muffin tin with plastic wrap or foil-laminated baking cups and press crust mix all around to sheathe the cups. Use your fingers (protecting them with plastic wrap if necessary) or use the back of a spoon to smooth and even out the crust. Three tablespoons will do the trick. Start with 2 tablespoons of crust mix and completely cover the sides of each baking cup with it, and then use the remaining tablespoon of the crust mix to cover the bottom of each cup. Refrigerate pan to firm up crusts. Label and freeze any leftover crust mix.

FILLING

½ pound (one 8-ounce package) cream cheese

⅔ cup sweetened condensed milk

⅓ cup fresh lime juice

1 large fresh peach or nectarine

⅓ cup ginger marmalade

Fruit Fresh

In a food processor, blend cream cheese, condensed milk, and lime juice together well. Cut fruit into slices and reserve a fourth of the fruit as garnish for the tops of the filled muffins. Add marmalade and fruit to batter and pulse on-off 5 times to chop slightly and fold in. Pour batter into crust cups. Sprinkle reserved peach slices with Fruit Fresh and insert one slice into the top of each muffin to decorate and identify them, in case you freeze some and later don't remember what flavor they are.

Grapefruit Nonbaked Cheesecake Muffins

We particularly like this flavor. We think it is subtle and elegant.

CRUST

- 5 tablespoons lightly salted butter
- 6 ounces white chocolate
- 1 cup finely chopped walnuts
- 1 cup finely chopped vanilla-wafer crumbs

Melt butter and chocolate together over simmering water in the top of a double boiler, or in a microwave oven at half power, and reserve. Blend crumbs and nuts together in a food processor and then add chocolate mixture and pulse until well combined. Line each cup of a muffin tin with plastic wrap or insert a foil-laminated baking cup, and press crust mix all around to sheathe it. Smooth and even out the crust. Three tablespoons of crust per muffin will do the trick. Refrigerate pan. Label and freeze any leftover crust mix.

FILLING

- 3 ounces white chocolate
- 11 ounces (one 8-ounce package + one 3-ounce package) cream cheese
- 1 cup sweetened condensed milk
- 2 tablespoons Fruit Fresh
- ¼ cup frozen grapefruit juice concentrate, undiluted
- 1½ tablespoons grapefruit extract or flavoring
- 2 tablespoons Fruit Fresh

Melt chocolate over simmering water in the top of a double boiler, or in a microwave oven on half power, and reserve. Process cream cheese and sweetened condensed milk in food processor until smooth and creamy. Dissolve Fruit Fresh in grapefruit juice. Add to processor along with melted white chocolate and extract, and blend well. Fill each crust cup with about ¼ cup of batter.

GARNISH

grapefruit-flavored jellied candies

canned drained or fresh grapefruit segments,
    sprinkled with Fruit Fresh

Decorate each muffin with a grapefruit-flavored jellied candy or a segment of fresh grapefruit. If you choose fresh grapefruit, sprinkle segments with Fruit Fresh to keep them from turning brown. Refrigerate to set.

Chocolate Raspberry Nonbaked Cheesecake Muffins

CRUST

4 tablespoons (½ stick) lightly salted butter

1 pound white, dark, or milk chocolate–covered
   pretzels

2 cups finely chopped walnuts

Melt butter and reserve, but use it while it is warm. Blend chocolate-covered pretzels and nuts together in a food processor and then add melted butter and pulse until well combined. Line each cup of a muffin tin with plastic wrap or insert a foil-laminated baking cup and press crust mix all around to sheathe it. Smooth and even out the crust. Three tablespoons of crust per muffin will do the trick. Refrigerate pan. Label and freeze any leftover crust mix.

FILLING

2 ounces dark chocolate

1 pound (2 8-ounce packages) cream cheese

1 cup sweetened condensed milk

⅔ cup frozen raspberry daiquiri concentrate,
   undiluted

Melt chocolate over simmering water in the top of a double boiler, or in a microwave oven on half power, and reserve. Process cream cheese, sweetened condensed milk, melted chocolate, and raspberry daiquiri concentrate in a food processor until smooth and creamy. Fill each crust cup with about ¼ cup of batter.

GARNISH

fresh raspberries sprinkled with Fruit Fresh

Decorate each muffin with a few fresh raspberries that have been sprinkled with Fruit Fresh to prevent them from turning brown. Refrigerate to set.

Irish Cream Nonbaked Cheesecake Muffins

CRUST

4 ounces dark chocolate

1 ounce white chocolate

3 tablespoons lightly salted butter

1 cup finely chopped shortbread crumbs

1 cup finely chopped Brazil nuts

Melt butter and both kinds of chocolate together over simmering water in the top of a double boiler, or in a microwave oven at half power, and reserve. Blend shortbread crumbs and nuts together in a food processor and then add butter/chocolate mixture and pulse until well combined. Line each cup of a muffin tin with plastic wrap or insert a foil-laminated baking cup and press crust mix all around to sheathe it. Smooth and even out the crust. Three tablespoons of crust per muffin will do the trick. Refrigerate pan. Label and freeze any leftover crust mix.

FILLING

3 ounces white chocolate

11 ounces (one 8-ounce + one 3-ounce package) cream cheese

⅔ cup sweetened condensed milk

2 tablespoons Irish Cream liqueur

1 teaspoon coffee extract

Melt chocolate over simmering water in the top of a double boiler, or in a microwave oven at half power, and reserve. Process cream cheese, sweetened condensed milk, melted chocolate, Irish Cream liqueur, and extract in a food processor until smooth and creamy. Fill each crust cup with about ¼ cup of batter.

GARNISH

shaved dark chocolate

Decorate each muffin with shaved chocolate and refrigerate to set.

Pretzel, Root Beer, and Jelly Bean Nonbaked Cheesecake Muffins

CRUST

- 6 tablespoons (¾ stick) lightly salted butter
- 6 ounces white chocolate
- 2 ounces dark, sweet, or semisweet chocolate
- 12 ounces pretzels, unsalted or with salt brushed off
- 1½ cups finely chopped Brazil nuts

Melt butter and both kinds of chocolate together over simmering water in the top of a double boiler, or in a microwave oven at half power, and reserve. Process pretzels, blend well with nuts in a food processor, and then add chocolate mixture and pulse until well combined. Line each cup of a muffin tin with plastic wrap or insert a foil-laminated baking cup and press crust mix all around to sheathe it. Smooth and even out the crust. Three tablespoons of crust per muffin will do the trick. Refrigerate pan. Label and freeze any leftover crust mix.

FILLING

- 3 ounces white chocolate
- 11 ounces (one 8-ounce package + one 3-ounce package) cream cheese
- ⅔ cup sweetened condensed milk
- 2 teaspoons Fruit Fresh
- 2 tablespoons frozen white grape juice concentrate, undiluted
- 2 tablespoons root beer flavoring
- 3 drops yellow food coloring

Melt chocolate over simmering water in the top of a double boiler, or in a microwave oven at half power, and reserve. Process cream cheese and sweetened condensed milk in a food processor until smooth and creamy. Dissolve

Fruit Fresh in grape juice. Add to processor with root beer flavoring, melted chocolate, and food coloring, and process till well combined. Fill each crust cup with about ¼ cup of batter.

GARNISH
jelly beans

Scatter jelly beans on top of each muffin and refrigerate to set.

Prune Danish Nonbaked Cheesecake Muffins

CRUST

¼ pound (1 stick) lightly salted butter

4 ounces white chocolate

1½ cups finely ground Danish butter-cookie crumbs

1½ cups finely chopped blanched almonds

Melt butter and chocolate together over simmering water in the top of a double boiler, or in a microwave oven at half power, and reserve. Blend cookie crumbs and nuts in a food processor, and then add chocolate mixture and pulse until well combined. Line each cup of a muffin tin with plastic wrap or insert a foil-laminated baking cup and press crust mix all around to sheathe it. Smooth and even out the crust. Three tablespoons of crust per muffin will do the trick. Refrigerate pan. Label and freeze any leftover crust mix.

FILLING

1 pound (2 8-ounce packages) cream cheese

⅓ cup fresh lemon juice

1 14-ounce can sweetened condensed milk

¼ cup prune cake filling or lekvar

Blend cream cheese, sweetened condensed milk, and lemon juice in a food processor until smooth and creamy. Spread 1 teaspoon of prune filling in the bottom of each muffin cup, then fill the cups with batter, about ¼ cup to each.

GARNISH

¼ cup prune cake filling or lekvar

Dab 1 teaspoon of prune filling in the center of each muffin so it looks like the topping of a Danish pastry. Refrigerate to set.

Amaretto Almond Nonbaked Cheesecake Muffins

We made these in individual ready-made store-bought crusts, which are acceptable only in the direst emergencies. This amount of batter will fill 6 individual ready-made crusts. If you use your own crusts, this amount of batter will fill 12.

CRUST

- ¼ pound (1 stick) lightly salted butter
- 4 ounces white chocolate
- 1½ cups finely ground shortbread crumbs
- 1½ cups finely chopped blanched almonds

Melt butter and chocolate together over simmering water in the top of a double boiler, or in a microwave oven at half power, and reserve. Blend shortbread crumbs and nuts in a food processor and then add chocolate mixture and pulse until well combined. Line each cup of a muffin tin with plastic wrap or insert a foil-laminated baking cup and press crust mix all around to sheathe it. Smooth and even out the crust. Three tablespoons of crust per muffin will do the trick. Refrigerate pan. Label and freeze any leftover crust mix.

FILLING

- 4 ounces white chocolate
- ½ pound (one 8-ounce package) cream cheese
- ⅔ cup sweetened condensed milk
- 2 teaspoons Fruit Fresh
- 1 tablespoon frozen orange juice concentrate, undiluted
- 3 tablespoons amaretto liqueur
- ¼ teaspoon almond extract
- ¾ cup sliced almonds, with skin

Melt chocolate over simmering water in the top of a double boiler, or in a microwave oven on half power, and reserve. Process cream cheese and sweetened condensed milk in a food processor until smooth and creamy. Dissolve Fruit Fresh in orange juice. Add to processor with amaretto, almond extract, and melted chocolate and process till well combined. Fold in nuts. Fill each crust cup with about ¼ cup of batter.

GARNISH
sliced almonds, with skin

Sprinkle almonds on top of each muffin and refrigerate to set.

Halloween Nonbaked Cheesecake Muffins

CRUST

9 tablespoons (1 stick + 1 tablespoon) lightly
  salted butter

8 ounces white chocolate

2 ounces dark chocolate

3 cups finely chopped caramel corn

1 cup chopped peanuts

Melt butter and both chocolates together over simmering water in the top of a double boiler, in a saucepan on a heat diffuser, or in a microwave oven on half power, and reserve. Chop up caramel corn and peanuts as finely as you can in a food processor. Don't be alarmed if you can't. This crust tends to be bulky. Add chocolate mixture and pulse until well combined. Line each cup of a muffin tin with plastic wrap or insert a foil-laminated baking cup and press crust mix all around to sheathe it. Smooth and even out the crust. Refrigerate pan. Label and freeze any leftover crust mix. (We made this in foil-laminated cups and they required a lot of crust. Don't be stingy.) The recipe produces lots of crust mix, so make the sides very firm. It might be helpful if you wrap your hand in plastic wrap and press each nugget of mix against the side of the processor bowl to flatten it before pressing it against the side of the foil cup.

FILLING

½ pound (one 8-ounce package) cream cheese

⅔ cup sweetened condensed milk

1 tablespoon Fruit Fresh

⅓ cup frozen orange juice concentrate, undiluted

5 dots red food coloring

10 dots yellow food coloring

Process cream cheese and sweetened condensed milk in a food processor until smooth and creamy. Dissolve Fruit Fresh in orange juice. Add to processor with food coloring and process till well combined. Fill crust cups with filling. Because these crusts are thick, they will need little more than ⅛ cup of filling.

GARNISH

12 pumpkin faces or other Halloween candies

Press one candy into middle of each muffin and refrigerate to set.

Chocolate Nut Nonbaked Cheesecake Muffins

CRUST

4½ tablespoons lightly salted butter

9 ounces chocolate nonpareils

¾ cup chopped shortbread crumbs

1½ cups chopped hazelnuts

Melt butter and chocolate nonpareils together over simmering water in the top of a double boiler, or in a microwave oven on half power, and reserve. Blend shortbread crumbs and nuts in a food processor and then add chocolate mixture and pulse until well combined. Line each cup of a muffin tin with plastic wrap or insert a foil-laminated baking cup and press crust mix all around to sheathe it. Smooth and even out the crust. Three tablespoons of crust per muffin will do the trick. Refrigerate pan. Label and freeze any leftover crust mix.

FILLING

3 ounces white chocolate

11 ounces (one 8-ounce package + one 3-ounce package) cream cheese

1 scant cup sweetened condensed milk

2 tablespoons crème de cacao

2 tablespoons praline liqueur

4 teaspoons Fruit Fresh

1½ tablespoons orange juice concentrate, undiluted

¾ cup coarsely chopped hazelnuts

2 ounces shaved semisweet chocolate

Melt white chocolate over simmering water in the top of a double boiler, or in a microwave oven on half power, and reserve. Process cream cheese, sweetened condensed milk, crème de cacao and praline liqueur in a food processor until smooth and creamy. Dissolve Fruit Fresh in orange juice. Add to processor and blend well. Fold in hazelnuts and shaved chocolate. Fill each crust cup with about ¼ cup of batter.

GARNISH

shaved chocolate

Sprinkle each muffin with shaved chocolate and refrigerate to set.

Basic Lemon-Lime Baked Cheesecake Muffins

Preheat oven to 350 degrees F. Ingredients need not be at room temperature. Line each muffin tin with a foil-laminated baking cup or cut a 1" × 7" strip of aluminum foil and run it across the bottom and sides of each muffin tin like a stirrup.

CRUST

¼ pound (1 stick) lightly salted butter

2 cups vanilla-wafer crumbs

¼ cup sugar

Melt butter over very low heat. Combine butter with crumbs and sugar in a food processor until thoroughly blended, or stir and mash together with a fork in a roomy bowl. Press small amounts of crust mix all the way up the sides of the ungreased muffin cups and then press over bottom.

BATTER

1 pound (2 8-ounce packages) cream cheese

¾ cup sugar

2½ teaspoons lime or lemon juice

2 large eggs

In a mixer or food processor, blend cream cheese and sugar well. Add lime or lemon juice and blend in thoroughly. Add the eggs, one at a time, on low speed in order to prevent too much air from destroying the proper consistency of the batter. Mix just until each egg has been incorporated into the batter. Pour batter into muffin crusts and bake in preheated oven for 8 minutes. Remove from oven and let stand on a counter for 2 minutes before putting on the glaze.

(cont'd)

SOUR-CREAM GLAZE

½ cup sour cream

1 tablespoon sugar

¼ teaspoon almond extract

Combine sour cream, sugar, and extract with a rubber spatula in a plastic bowl. Spread evenly and smoothly over tops of muffins and return to 350 degree F. oven for 2 minutes. Remove from oven and **immediately** place in refrigerator to cool. If you haven't lined each cup with a baking cup, let cupcakes stand at room temperature for a few minutes to allow the butter to loosen its bond with the metal. Separate the sides from the metal with a warm sharp knife and pull up on the foil stirrups. The crust will usually detach easily from the sides.

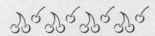

BONUS!

Baked Cheesecake Muffins Magic Formula

You can make muffins from any of our baked cheesecake recipes. For each dozen, here's the magic formula:

Preheat oven to 350 degrees F. Ingredients need not be at room temperature. Line each muffin tin with a foil-laminated baking cup or cut a 1" × 7" strip of aluminum foil and run it across the bottom and side of each muffin tin like a stirrup.

CRUST

¼ pound (1 stick) lightly salted butter
2 cups finely ground cookie crumbs
¼ cup sugar

Melt butter over very low heat. Combine butter with crumbs and sugar in a food processor until thoroughly blended, or stir and mash together with a fork in a roomy bowl. Press small amounts of crust mix all the way up the sides and over the bottoms of the ungreased muffin cups.

BATTER

1 pound (2 8-ounce packages) cream cheese
1 cup sugar

1½ tablespoons flavoring juice

½ teaspoon extract or liqueur

pinch of salt

2 large eggs

In a mixer or food processor, blend cream cheese and sugar well. Add juice, extract, and salt, and blend in thoroughly. Add the eggs, one at a time, on low speed in order to prevent too much air from destroying the proper consistency of the batter. Mix just until each egg has been incorporated into the batter. Pour batter into muffin crusts and bake in preheated oven for 8 minutes. Remove from oven and let stand on a counter for 2 minutes before putting on the glaze. If you don't want to bother with a glaze, refrigerate muffins after they sit on the countertop for 2 minutes.

SOUR-CREAM GLAZE

½ cup sour cream

1 tablespoon sugar

¼ teaspoon extract

This recipe should provide you with a tablespoon or so of glaze for each of the dozen muffins. Bake for 2 minutes more in a preheated oven and refrigerate.

LOWER-CALORIE CHEESECAKES

Ten Tricks for Lowering the Calorie and Fat Content of Cheesecakes

Let's not kid ourselves. If God had wanted cheesecake to be a diet aid, He would have made butterfat noncaloric. We hope you've noticed that we hid that unpleasant fact toward the end of the book, where you really have to dig to find it. However, cheesecakes can be less caloric if you have a few tricks up your sleeve, and can think fearlessly. They will not taste as rich and as sweet as the ones you've read about on previous pages, but they will be quite edible and far less guilt-producing.

ESSENTIAL WORKING TOOLS AND NECESSARY IMPLEMENTS
The tools you'll need include a surgical mask (not for purity, but to keep your mouth off-limits). Working in rubber gloves is also helpful. We've never seen any cook lick batter off those. A sink full of soapy water is another must, so you can defile your mixing pans before that leftover batter defiles your lips. Remember, only skinny blondes with thick, straight hair are born loving low-calorie wonders like apricots, coffee, and raspberries. The rest of us must acquire a taste for them—and never really prefer them to fudge.

You'll need a food processor, to whip the blazes out of whatever inferior substitute you're using to replace the more caloric and tastier cream cheese, so that even if you have far less butterfat than in a regular cheesecake, at least you'll have the same texture and appearance.

TRICK NUMBER ONE

Despite what you may secretly believe, *all* cookie crumbs are high in calories. We thought there were big differences, and that zwieback had lots fewer calories than vanilla wafers because it tastes dry and gritty. No way. The cookie-crumb maven at Nabisco told us it ain't so. Cookies crumble at the rate of 400 to 600 calories per cup. Here's proof positive from the horse's mouth:

CALORIES IN ONE CUP OF
VARIOUS FINELY GROUND COOKIE CRUMBS

Chocolate sandwich cookies = 611 calories

Gingersnaps = 540 calories

Chocolate-chip cookies = 517 calories

Shortbread = 490 calories

Vanilla wafers = 475 calories

Chocolate wafers = 468 calories

Graham crackers = 420 calories

Zwieback = 400 calories

Read 'em and weep.

We suppose you could make a crust out of colored, flavored sawdust, but there *is* a tastier solution. Make your crust out of cereal crumbs. They're sweet but somewhat lower in calories, and if they're loaded with additives and preservatives, so are the higher-calorie cookie crumbs. To give you an idea of the difference, for an 8-inch cheesecake made with one pound of whatever cheese, you need about 1¼ cups of crumbs. The cereal crumbs tally about 110 calories per ounce, which grind down to 220 calories per cup. You don't have to be a math major to see the saving in calories. You can forgo any additional sugar (just add two packs of artificial sweetener if you feel the need), but you can't forgo one crumb. You have to really press the crust mixture into the sides and dig out any excess from the angle where the sides meet the bottom. The best way to make these crusts go farther is to smooth them and even them by fitting in a sheet of plastic wrap and pressing the crusts under it with the back of a spoon. And here's a surprise for you: Caramel corn and Cracker Jack contain only 110 calories per ounce. Caramel corn grinds up into a 110-calorie cup of crumbs. We got so excited, we tried it in a crust—but nothing is perfect. It was very gummy, and we didn't like working with it. We prefer sweet, crunchy, hard cereals like Honey Nut Cheerios and Cocoa Puffs.

TRICK NUMBER TWO

Instead of using butter or margarine (100 calories per tablespoon) to bind the crumbs together, a dieter can make do with only 3 or 4 tablespoons of a light butter or margarine (50 to 60 calories per tablespoon) or Le Slim Cow (only 56 calories per tablespoon), which contains buttermilk. We prefer Land O Lakes Country Morning Blend Light because the taste and texture are more traditional, but we've used them all, and any will do. Just make sure you give yourself the whole 200-calorie amount.

However, if you want to cut even more calories, make the cheesecake in a pie pan sprayed with vegetable-oil spray instead of a springform pan, and use only ⅓ cup cereal crumbs. Swirl the crumbs around so that a thin layer sticks to the sides of the pan, and spread the rest evenly over the bottom. The cheesecake batter will combine with the cereal and supply a somewhat undefined crust. Or eliminate the crumbs altogether and make the cheesecake in a vegetable oil–sprayed pan.

TRICK NUMBER THREE

Make sure the fat really blends into the cereal crumbs in the processor and doesn't stick to the bottom of the bowl, so your crusts get every bit of butterfat they are entitled to. And remember: The warmer the crumbs are, the more manageable they will be.

TRICK NUMBER FOUR

Stay away from whole eggs. We usually substitute 3 egg whites (17 calories each) for every 2 whole eggs (81 calories each) in a recipe. In addition to slightly reduced calories, you get monumentally reduced cholesterol. We see no reason to use cholesterol-free real egg products in cheesecake. They're just frozen, colored egg whites. You have to defrost them, and they cost a whole lot more.

TRICK NUMBER FIVE

Initially, we add half the amount of sugar we think a batter really requires to sweeten it properly, and then we make up the difference with artificial sweeteners. There's one on the market called Sunette Sweet One Low-Calorie-Sugar Substitute, which is sodium-free and heat stable and hadn't created any diseases in its users when we turned in this manuscript, although since then it's been shown to increase blood-cholesterol levels in diabetic test animals, so avoid feeding it to your diabetic pets.

We like the taste of sugar, but if you don't, here are a few other substitutes you might employ. Fructose comes from the natural sugar found in fresh fruits and honey. It's approximately 50 percent sweeter than table sugar and is metabolized differently in the body. Unlike sugar, which passes through the liver and enters the bloodstream immediately, causing a rise in blood sugar level, fructose is trapped in the liver and stored as carbohydrate. It enters the bloodstream very gradually. Because it causes less of an increase in blood sugar, it's acceptable for diabetics—up to 75 grams can be consumed by them per day, as long as it's accounted for on an exchange basis: that is, 1 teaspoon of fructose is equal to the carbohydrate portion of ½ fruit exchange. One cup of sugar has 960 calories. A comparably sweet amount of fructose (¾ cup) has a mere 550 calories.

Another possible substitute is Sucanat, which has 12 calories per teaspoon, as opposed to 20 in sugar, and tallies up to 576 calories per cup. It's simply evaporated cane juice.

If you wish to cut your sugar intake, taste these substitutes and use your favorite.

For artificial sweeteners, we use Sunette Sweet One in our baked low-calorie cheesecakes, but we prefer Equal in the unbaked cheesecakes. We like the flavor better, but Equal loses its sweetness when it's heated for a long period of time, so it's not ideal for baking.

TRICK NUMBER SIX

Pure cream cheese is too fattening. Here's a list of possible substitutes:

CHEESE	CALORIES PER OUNCE	CALORIES PER POUND
Cream cheese	100	1600
Light cream cheese or Neufchatel	80	1280
Imitation cream cheese	60	960
Part-skim ricotta	45	720
Farmer cheese	40	640
Cottage cheese	30	480
Low-fat cottage cheese (2%)	23	368
Low-fat yogurt, drained overnight in a cone (8 ounces = 6½ ounces yogurt cheese)	23	368
Light n' Lively or other 1% cottage cheese	20	320

The trick with all of these is to really whip the blazes out of them in a food processor so that they acquire the texture of cream cheese. Then sweeten them enough to conceal the blandness that results from the reduction of fat. You can use one kind of cheese for each cake, or blend them together. Mix them and match them. It doesn't really matter as long as the proportions stay the same. They should bake in the same amount of time. You can even make nonbaked cakes with them!

TRICK NUMBER SEVEN
Always make these lower-calorie cheesecakes in an 8-inch springform pan so your crumbs will go farther. Top them with sliced fresh fruit to make them look grand and elegant.

TRICK NUMBER EIGHT
Add fresh ripe fruits to the batter to extend the flavor without increasing the caloric value very much.

TRICK NUMBER NINE

Except for fresh fruit, toppings are out! They're just too expensive calorie-wise, and really not necessary. Make the cake look fattening and beautiful by sprinkling on cocoa or a smidgen of grated chocolate right before serving, or something equally mouth-watering, yet deceptive. As a last resort, there's always the tried-and-true disguise: powdering the top with confectioners' sugar so people will think they're eating something mah-velous.

TRICK NUMBER TEN

Make as small a cake as possible. Always make less than you think you'll need. You never want leftover cheesecake, even the low-cal kind, singing a siren song to you from the refrigerator 'round about midnight.

Turn the page and see how these tricks actually work in practice. You'll have to follow instructions on these and blot and drain when we say so, because otherwise the cakes will be too watery and they won't cook fast enough.

LOWER-CALORIE CHEESECAKE

RECIPES

Lower-Calorie Pineapple Cheesecake

Preheat oven to 350 degrees F. Coat a 10-inch springform pan with vegetable-oil spray.

CRUST

¼ cup (4 tablespoons) reduced-fat margarine

1¼ cups crumbs from crispy brown rice cereal

1 tablespoon sugar

2 packets heat-stable artificial sweetener

Melt margarine over very low heat, add it to the crumbs, sugar, and sweetener in a food processor, and blend till well combined. Put all the crust mix in your springform pan and wrap plastic wrap over your fingers to help press the mix around the sides to a height of no more than 1 inch. Press remaining crust mix over the bottom of your pan. It may not stick perfectly, but do the best you can. We generally press it to a height of 1 inch against the sides and then use the back of a spoon to spread it onto the bottom, stealing from the sides until we have enough to cover the bottom. Set aside.

BATTER AND GARNISH

- 8 ounces light cream cheese or Neufchatel cheese
- 8 ounces part-skim-milk ricotta cheese
- 1 teaspoon pineapple extract
- ¼ cup sugar
- 8 packets heat-stable artificial sweetener
- 2 large egg whites
- ½ ounce sugarless dried or fresh pineapple, very thinly sliced

Blot excess water from cheeses with a paper towel. Whip up cheeses, extract, sugar, and artificial sweetener in food processor until very creamy. Add egg whites and whip in with 5 to 7 on-off pulses. Fold in pineapple and pour into crust. Bake for 25 minutes in preheated oven. Cool in refrigerator. Decorate with thinly sliced dried sugarless pineapple or fresh pineapple slices.

Cory's Old-Fashioned Light Cheesecake

Preheat oven to 350 degrees F. Coat an 8-inch springform pan with vegetable-oil spray.

CRUST

- ¼ cup (4 tablespoons) reduced-fat margarine
- 1½ cups fine Honeycomb (or similar) cereal crumbs
- 2 tablespoons sugar
- 3 packets heat-stable artificial sweetener
- 1 teaspoon cinnamon
- 1 tablespoon chopped toasted almonds

Melt margarine over very low heat; add it to the crumbs, sugar, artificial sweetener, and cinnamon in a food processor; and blend until well combined. Mix ¼-cup crumbs with nuts and reserve to sprinkle on top of baked cake. Put all the rest of the crust mix into the springform pan and wrap plastic wrap over your fingers to help press the mix around the sides to the height of 1½ inches. Then press remaining crust mix over the bottom of your pan. Set aside.

BATTER AND GARNISH

- ¾ pound farmer cheese
- 4 ounces Neufchatel or light cream cheese
- ¼ cup sugar
- 6 packets heat-stable artificial sweetener
- 1 teaspoon vanilla extract
- 1 teaspoon rum extract
- ½ teaspoon black walnut extract
- 4 large egg whites
- confectioners' sugar for garnish

Blot excess liquid from cheeses with paper towel. Whip up cheeses, sugar, sweetener, and extracts in a food processor until very smooth and creamy. When you think it looks and acts like cream cheese, process it for 10 seconds more. Add egg whites and blend until just incorporated—15 on-off pulses. Pour into crust and bake for 20 minutes in preheated oven. Sprinkle reserved crust on top and refrigerate at once to cool. Sprinkle with confectioners' sugar before serving.

Lower-Calorie Butter-Caramel-Nut Cheesecake

Preheat oven to 350 degrees F. Coat an 8-inch springform pan with vegetable-oil spray.

CRUST

- 3 tablespoons reduced-fat margarine
- 1½ cups Crunchy Nut Ohs (or similar) cereal crumbs
- 1 tablespoon sugar
- 2 packets heat-stable artificial sweetener

Melt margarine over very low heat; add it to the crumbs, sugar, and sweetener in a food processor; and blend till well combined. Put all the crumbs into the springform pan and wrap plastic wrap over your fingers to help press the mix around the sides to the height of no more than 1 inch. Then press remaining crust mix over the bottom of your pan. Set aside.

BATTER AND GARNISH

- 8 ounces part-skim-milk ricotta cheese
- 8 ounces Neufchatel cheese
- ¼ cup sugar
- 6 packets heat-stable artificial sweetener
- ¾ teaspoon caramel extract
- ½ teaspoon butterscotch extract
- 2 large egg whites
- 1 tablespoon slivered almonds
- 1 tablespoon caramel ice-cream topping

Blot excess liquid from cheeses with a paper towel. Blend cheeses, sugar, sweetener, and extracts in food processor until very creamy. Add egg whites and whip in quickly with 5 to 7 on-off pulses. Pour into crust. Bake for 22 minutes in preheated oven. Sprinkle almonds on top, dribble caramel topping around them, and refrigerate.

Lower-Calorie Apricot Cheesecake

Preheat oven to 350 degrees F. Coat an 8-inch springform pan with vegetable-oil spray.

CRUST

¼ cup (4 tablespoons) reduced-fat margarine

1½ cups crumbs from a sweet, crunchy cereal

1 tablespoon sugar

2 packages heat-stable artificial sweetener

Melt margarine over very low heat; add it to the crumbs, sugar, and sweetener in a food processor; and blend till well combined. Reserve 1 tablespoon crust mix for topping. Put all the crumbs in the springform pan and wrap plastic wrap over your fingers to help press the mix around the sides to the height of no more than 1 inch. Then press remaining mix over the bottom of the pan. Set aside.

BATTER AND GARNISH

1 8-ounce can low-calorie apricot halves

1 pound farmer cheese

⅓ cup sugar

3 packets heat-stable artificial sweetener

1½ teaspoons brandy extract

3 large egg whites

¼ cup low-calorie apricot preserves

Drain and blot apricot halves. Discard syrup, reserve three halves for topping, and cut the remainder into chunks. Process cheese, sugar, sweetener, and 1¼ teaspoons extract until very smooth. Add egg whites and apricot chunks and whip into batter in 7 on-off pulses. Pour into crust. Slice reserved apricots in long, thin slices and decorate top of cake. Sprinkle with reserved crust-mix crumbs. Bake for 20 minutes in preheated oven. Put into refrigerator to cool. When cool, process ¼ cup low-calorie apricot preserves with ¼ teaspoon brandy extract and glaze top of cake with a brush.

Lower-Calorie Vermont Apple Cheesecake

Preheat oven to 350 degrees F. Coat an 8-inch springform pan with vegetable-oil spray.

CRUST

- 3½ tablespoons reduced-fat margarine
- 1½ cups crumbs from Apple Jacks cereal
- 1 tablespoon sugar
- 2 packets heat-stable artificial sweetener
- 1 teaspoon cinnamon

Melt margarine over very low heat; add it to the crumbs, sugar, sweetener, and cinnamon in a food processor; and blend till well combined. Put all the crumbs into the springform pan and wrap plastic wrap over your fingers to help press the mix around the sides to the height of no more than 1 inch. Then press remaining mix over the bottom of the pan. Set aside.

BATTER

- 8 ounces Neufchatel cheese
- 4 ounces farmer cheese
- 4 ounces part-skim-milk ricotta cheese
- ¼ cup sugar
- 3 packets heat-stable artificial sweetener
- ¾ teaspoon maple flavoring
- 2 large egg whites
- 1 pack Weight Watchers dried apple snacks
- ½ teaspoon cinnamon

Blend cheeses, sugar, sweetener, and maple flavoring in food processor until very creamy. Whip in egg whites with 7 to 10 on-off pulses. Dredge apple snacks in cinnamon and fold into batter. Pour into crust. Bake for 20 minutes in preheated oven. Cool in refrigerator.

Lower-Calorie Mocha Mist Cheesecake

Preheat oven to 350 degrees F. Coat an 10-inch springform pan with vegetable-oil spray.

CRUST

3½   tablespoons reduced-fat margarine

1½   cups chocolate-cereal crumbs

  1   tablespoon sugar

  2   packets heat-stable artificial sweetener

Melt margarine and combine with all other ingredients in a food processor.
Press mixture ¾ inch up sides of the springform pan and then press and
smooth remainder over bottom. Set aside.

BATTER AND GARNISH

  8   ounces imitation cream cheese

  8   ounces low-fat cottage cheese, drained well

 ¼   cup nonfat dry milk

  1   teaspoon instant coffee

 ¾   teaspoon coffee extract

 ¼   teaspoon vanilla

 ¼   cup sugar

  8   packages heat-stable artificial sweetener

  2   large egg whites

  1   ounce mocha-flavored chocolate

Blend together all ingredients except for egg whites in food processor until
very smooth and creamy. Add egg whites. Blend in with 10 on-off pulses.
Pour into crust and bake for 30 minutes in preheated oven. Refrigerate. When
chilled, grate mocha-flavored chocolate on top.

Lower-Calorie Nonbaked
Lemon-Lime-Mint Cheesecake

Coat an 8-inch springform pan with vegetable-oil spray.

CRUST

¼ cup (4 tablespoons) reduced-fat margarine
1½ cups crumbs from a crunchy sweet cereal
3 packages artificial sweetener
1 tablespoon sugar
½ teaspoon cinnamon

Melt margarine. Add to all other ingredients in a food processor and process until thoroughly blended. Press 1 inch around sides and sprinkle the remainder over the bottom of the springform pan.

FILLING

1 pound low-fat cottage cheese, drained well
⅓ cup sweetened condensed milk
12 packets artificial sweetener
2 tablespoons fresh lime juice
1 tablespoon fresh lemon juice
½ teaspoon lemon extract
½ teaspoon lime extract
1 teaspoon dried mint

Blend cottage cheese, sweetened condensed milk, and artificial sweetener in food processor until thoroughly blended and smooth. Add juices, extracts, and mint to batter and whip until well blended. Pour into crust and refrigerate until set.

Lower-Calorie Nonbaked Tropical Fruit Cheesecake

Coat an 8-inch springform pan with vegetable-oil spray.

CRUST

3½ tablespoons reduced-fat margarine

1½ cups cereal crumbs from a sweet, crisp cereal

1 tablespoon sugar

2 packets artificial sweetener

Melt margarine. Add to crumbs, sugar, and artificial sweetener in processor and process until well blended. Press 1½ inch up sides and pat down over bottom of springform pan.

FILLING

1 pound low-fat cottage cheese, drained
   and blotted

⅓ cup sweetened condensed milk

2 teaspoons Fruit Fresh

3 tablespoons tropical-blend juice concentrate,
   undiluted

1 tablespoon fresh lemon juice

½ teaspoon guava extract

½ teaspoon passion-fruit extract

6 packets artificial sweetener

Blend cottage cheese and sweetened condensed milk together in food processor. Dissolve Fruit Fresh in juices and add to food processor along with extracts and artificial sweetener; blend well to combine. Pour into crust and refrigerate until set.

Lower-Calorie Orange Mocha Nonbaked Cheesecake

Coat a 10-inch springform pan with vegetable-oil spray.

CRUST
¼ cup (4 tablespoons) reduced-fat margarine

1½ cups crumbs from a chocolate cereal

1 tablespoon sugar

2 packets artificial sweetener

1½ teaspoons cinnamon

Melt margarine. Blend thoroughly with crumbs, sugar, sweetener, and cinnamon in food processor. Press mixture ¾ inch up the sides of the springform pan, then sprinkle remaining crumbs over bottom of pan.

FILLING
½ pound imitation cream cheese,
  drained and blotted

½ pound part-skim-milk ricotta cheese,
  drained and blotted

⅓ cup sweetened condensed milk

4 teaspoons Fruit Fresh

3 tablespoons frozen orange juice concentrate,
  undiluted

2 tablespoons cocoa

6 packets artificial sweetener

1 teaspoon mocha extract

Blend cheeses and condensed milk in food processor until smooth and creamy. Dissolve Fruit Fresh in orange juice and add to processor with cocoa, artificial sweetener, and mocha extract. Process until well blended. Pour into crust and put into refrigerator to set.

(cont'd)

GARNISH

1½ tablespoons cocoa

1 package artificial sweetener

Combine cocoa with artificial sweetener and sprinkle on top of cake for decoration.

Lower-Calorie Nonbaked Raspberry Daiquiri Cheesecake

Coat an 8-inch springform pan with vegetable-oil spray.

CRUST

¼ cup (4 tablespoons) reduced-fat margarine
1¼ cups crumbs from a crunchy, sweet cereal
1 tablespoon sugar
3 packages artificial sweetener
½ teaspoon cinnamon

Warm margarine slightly. Add to all other ingredients in a food processor and process until thoroughly blended. Press 1½ inches up the sides and sprinkle over bottom of the springform pan.

FILLING

12 ounces dry-flake cottage cheese
4 ounces small-curd cottage cheese, drained and blotted
⅓ cup sweetened condensed milk
12 packets artificial sweetener
3 tablespoons frozen raspberry daiquiri mix concentrate, undiluted
1 tablespoon lime juice
2 teaspoons Fruit Fresh
1½ cups fresh raspberries

Process cheeses, sweetened condensed milk, and artificial sweetener in food processor until thoroughly blended and smooth. Dissolve Fruit Fresh in juices, add to batter, and process until well blended. Distribute raspberries over crust, smooth batter over them, and refrigerate until set.

(cont'd)

GARNISH
fresh raspberries
Fruit Fresh

Sprinkle raspberries with Fruit Fresh and garnish top of cake with them.

CHAPTER

12

OTHER PEOPLE'S CHEESECAKES

$\mathcal{T}$he following recipes are for cheesecakes that we've also enjoyed when we tasted them at houses of friends—at least enough to have requested the recipe. So we're passing them on to you.

For Any Bakers Who Are Afraid of
Separating Eggs and Whipping Egg Whites

1. Separate the whites from the yolks when the eggs are cold.
2. Put the egg whites in a warmed mixing bowl.
3. Attach the wire whisk to your mixer and begin beating the egg whites on the lowest speed. Always beat egg whites with a wire whisk.
4. When the egg whites become frothy, add ⅛ teaspoon cream of tartar and continue to beat the whites until they peak. Egg whites traditionally should be whipped in a copper bowl. The cream of tartar replaces some of the minerals imparted to the egg whites from the copper. Copper bowls that fit

into mixer bowls are available from most kitchen-supply stores. Egg whites whip up beautifully in them using just the wire whisk.

5. To fold in remaining batter, add batter gradually to the egg whites in the bowl. The wire whisk on the lowest speed will blend them in beautifully.

Classic Lemon Cheesecake

Preheat oven to 500 degrees F. Grease and flour a 9-inch springform pan.

CRUST

2½ cups finely ground gingersnap crumbs
½ cup finely chopped pecans
⅓ cup sugar
1 stick lightly salted butter, softened

Combine crumbs, nuts, and sugar in a food processor. Cut the butter into 8 pieces and blend in well. Press the mixture over the bottom and up the sides of springform. Refrigerate.

BATTER

2½ pounds (5 8-ounce packages) cream cheese
at room temperature
1¾ cups sugar
3 tablespoons flour
1½ teaspoons grated lemon zest
1 teaspoon lemon juice
5 large eggs
2 egg yolks
¼ cup heavy cream
1 lemon, thinly sliced into semicircles

In food processor, cream together the cheese and the sugar. Add flour, lemon zest, and lemon juice and process for 2 minutes more. Blend in the eggs, one at a time, the egg yolks, and the cream. Remove the springform pan from the refrigerator and pour the batter into the crust. Bake for 10 minutes at 500 F., then reduce the oven temperature to 250 F. and bake 50 minutes longer. Let the cake cool thoroughly on a rack. Arrange the lemon slices around the rim of the top to form a border. Refrigerate for several hours, preferably overnight, before serving.

French Poppyseed Cheesecake

Preheat oven to 350 degrees F. Butter sides and bottom of a 9-inch springform pan.

CRUST

2 cups finely ground zwieback crumbs

¼ cup (4 tablespoons) melted butter

2 tablespoons sugar

Combine crumbs, sugar, and butter in a food processor until well blended. Press firmly around sides and bottom of springform pan.

BATTER

1 pound (2 8-ounce packages) cream cheese, softened

1½ tablespoons fresh lime juice

1 tablespoon grated lime zest

¾ cup sugar

4 tablespoons flour

1 teaspoon salt

1½ tablespoons poppyseed filling

4 eggs, separated

⅛ teaspoon cream of tartar (if egg whites are not whipped in a copper bowl)

1 cup heavy cream

In a mixer cream the cream cheese with the lime juice and zest, ½ cup sugar, flour, salt, and poppyseed. Add egg yolks and beat thoroughly. In a separate bowl with the wire whisk attachment beat the egg whites and optional cream of tartar until almost stiff. Gradually add the remaining ¼ cup sugar and beat until stiff and glossy. Fold the whipped egg whites into the cheese mixture thoroughly by using the wire whisk on the lowest speed. Fold in heavy cream. Pour into prepared crust. Bake in the preheated oven for 1½ hours. Refrigerate overnight. Serve chilled, but not ice cold.

Chocolate Pecan Cheesecake

Preheat oven to 325 degrees F. Grease sides only of a 10-inch springform pan.

CRUST

¾ cup finely ground vanilla-wafer crumbs

5 tablespoons melted butter

2 tablespoons sugar

2 tablespoons grated sweet chocolate

Combine all the ingredients in a food processor. Press the mixture firmly into the *bottom only* of a 10-inch, side-greased springform pan.

BATTER

3 eggs

1 cup sugar

1½ pounds (3 8-ounce packages) cream cheese,
   at room temperature

12 ounces sweet chocolate, grated in food
   processor.

1 cup sour cream

¾ cup butter

1 teaspoon vanilla extract

1 cup pecans, coarsely chopped

whipped cream (optional)

In mixer, beat the eggs and sugar until ribbons form when the beater is lifted. In another bowl, whip the cream cheese until very soft. Add the egg mixture to the cheese and beat on low speed until well combined. In the top of a double boiler, over boiling water, combine the chocolate, sour cream, butter, and vanilla. Cook, stirring, until the chocolate is melted and then blend into the cheese mixture. Fold in the pecans. Pour the batter into the crust and bake in the preheated oven for 2 hours. Cool on a wire rack, then remove from the pan. Refrigerate for 12 hours. Serve with whipped cream.

Marble Cheesecake

Preheat oven to 400 degrees F.

CRUST

¾ cup flour

2 tablespoons sugar

¼ teaspoon salt

¼ cup sweet butter

6 ounces sweet chocolate

Melt chocolate over simmering water in a double boiler or in a microwave oven on half power and reserve.

Combine flour, sugar, salt, and butter in a food processor until well blended. Add 2 tablespoons chocolate and blend until chocolate is incorporated. Press mixture into bottom and up sides of a 10″ springform pan. Bake at 400 degree F. for 10 minutes, then remove from oven and reduce oven temperature to 325 degree F.

BATTER

1½ pounds (3 8-ounce packages) cream cheese

1 cup sugar

¼ cup flour

1 teaspoon vanilla extract

6 eggs, separated

⅛ teaspoon cream of tartar (if egg whites are not
   whipped in a copper bowl)

1 cup sour cream

1 teaspoon coffee-flavored liqueur
   remainder of melted chocolate not used in
   crust

Soften cream cheese in food processor. Add sugar, flour, vanilla, and egg yolks and combine well. Blend in sour cream quickly on lowest speed. Reserve ¼ cup of batter.

In a mixer with wire whisk, beat egg whites until stiff. Fold in cheese mixture by switching to lowest speed and blending in with wire whisk attachment. Pour into crust. Add coffee-flavored liqueur and remaining melted chocolate to the reserved ¼ cup of batter. Pour chocolate into center of the white batter and cut through to achieve a marble effect. Bake in 325 degree F. oven for 1 hour. Turn off oven and allow cake to remain in oven for 30 minutes before removing. Refrigerate overnight.

French Lime Cheesecake

Preheat oven to 350 degrees F.

CRUST

1 box finely ground brown-edge wafers
½ cup lightly salted butter, melted
¼ cup sugar

Mix all ingredients together in a food processor or in a bowl with a fork. Press mixture over bottom and up sides of a 10-inch springform pan. Put a triple thickness of aluminum foil under and up sides of springform pan because cake is baked in a water-filled outside pan and the aluminum foil will keep the water from getting into the cake.

BATTER

3 pounds (6 8-ounce packages) cream cheese, softened
2½ cups sugar
6 eggs
½ cup plus 2 tablespoons flour
1½ cups heavy cream
1 teaspoon vanilla
¼ cup lime juice

Beat cream cheese in mixer. Add all the other ingredients one at a time, keeping mixer on lowest speed and mixing until well blended. Pour into crust. Place springform in a pan which is slightly larger and filled with 1 inch of boiling water (be careful not to scald yourself). Bake for 1 hour. Then turn off oven and let cake remain in oven for 30 minutes with the oven door closed.

Refrigerate overnight.

Chocolate Sin Cheesecake

Preheat oven to 350 degrees F.

CRUST
2 cups finely ground chocolate-wafer crumbs

2 tablespoons sugar

⅓ cup melted butter

pinch of salt

½ teaspoon cinnamon

Combine crumbs, sugar, butter, salt, and cinnamon and mix well. Press mixture firmly into the sides and over bottom of a 10-inch springform pan and chili for 30 minutes.

BATTER
12 ounces sweet chocolate

1½ pounds (3 8-ounce packages) cream cheese, at room temperature

1 cup sugar

3 eggs

2 tablespoons sweet butter, melted

2 cups heavy cream

1 teaspoon vanilla

Melt chocolate in a double boiler over simmering water, or in a microwave oven on half power, and reserve. In a mixer, beat cream cheese with sugar until fluffy; add eggs one by one, using the lowest speed of the mixer, just incorporating each egg before adding another. Add melted chocolate; then butter, cream, and vanilla; and mix until blended on low speed of mixer. Pour into springform pan. Bake 45 minutes until sides are firm. Cool, then chill in springform pan overnight.

Rich 'n' Creamy Lime Cheesecake

Preheat oven to 275 degrees F. Butter a 10-inch springform pan and dust with ½ cup finely ground vanilla-wafer crumbs.

BATTER

1 pound (2 8-ounce packages) cream cheese
4 tablespoons flour
1 tablespoon arrowroot
¾ cup sugar
1 large egg
½ teaspoon salt
½ tablespoon butter
1 tablespoon lime juice
1 teaspoon grated lime zest
6 tablespoons sour cream
1 cup milk
4 egg whites
⅛ teaspoon cream of tartar (if egg whites are not
   whipped in copper bowl)

In a mixer, whip cream cheese. Add flour, arrowroot, ½ cup of the sugar, egg, salt, butter, lime juice and zest. Beat on low speed for 2 minutes. Continue beating and add sour cream and milk. In a separate bowl, with wire whisk attachment whip egg whites to a soft peak. Add the remaining ¼ cup sugar and whip until stiff. Fold in cheese mixture on lowest speed of mixer with wire whisk and pour into the springform pan. Bake in the preheated oven for 2 hours. Refrigerate.

TOPPING

2 cups sour cream
¼ cup confectioners' sugar
1 teaspoon almond extract

Invert cake. Combine sour cream, sugar, and extract. Spread over cheesecake. Refrigerate until serving.

Angelic Cheesecake

Preheat oven to 350 degrees F. Butter a 10-inch springform pan with 2 tablespoons softened butter.

CRUST

¾ cup finely ground spiced-wafer crumbs

2 tablespoons sugar

6 tablespoons sweet butter, melted

In a food processor, combine crumbs, sugar, and melted butter. Sprinkle an even layer of the crumb mixture on the bottom and sides of the pan to form a shell. Refrigerate crust while you make the batter.

BATTER

1½ pounds cream cheese (3 8-ounce packages), softened

1½ cups sugar

6 eggs, separated

⅛ teaspoon cream of tartar (if egg whites are not whipped in copper bowl)

2 cups sour cream

3 tablespoons flour

1½ teaspoons triple sec

½ teaspoon vanilla extract

1 tablespoon lime juice

1 tablespoon finely grated lime zest

2 tablespoons confectioners' sugar

Beat the cream cheese in a mixer, then gradually beat in the sugar. Add the egg yolks, one at a time, on a low speed and continue to beat until thoroughly blended. Stir in the sour cream, flour, triple sec, vanilla, lime juice, and zest.

With the wire whisk of the mixer, beat the egg whites and optional cream of tartar until they are stiff. Fold in the cheese mixture with the wire whisk on the lowest speed until no streaks of white show.

Pour the batter into the prepared pan, spreading it out evenly with a rubber spatula. Bake in the middle of the preheated oven for 1 hour. Then turn off the oven, and with the oven door open, let the cake rest on the oven shelf for 15 minutes. Remove and cool to room temperature. Refrigerate. Before serving, sprinkle with confectioners' sugar.

Pumpkin Cheesecake

Preheat oven to 350 degrees F.

CRUST

3 cups finely ground spiced-wafer crumbs
½ cup confectioners' sugar
12 tablespoons butter, melted

Combine crumbs, sugar, and butter in a food processor and then spread on bottom and all the way up the sides of a 10″ ungreased springform pan.

BATTER

2½ pounds (5 8-ounce packages) cream cheese
3 eggs
1½ cups sugar
1 teaspoon vanilla extract
1 cup canned pumpkin
¼ cup dark rum
1½ teaspoons cinnamon
¼ teaspoon ground cloves
¼ teaspoon ground ginger
¼ teaspoon mace

Cream the cream cheese in a mixer on medium speed. Add eggs, sugar, and vanilla and beat until well incorporated. Add pumpkin, rum, and spices, blending thoroughly. Pour into crust and bake in the preheated oven for 1½ hours. Remove from oven.

Increase oven temperature to 500 degrees F.

TOPPING

2 cups sour cream
1 cup brown sugar
1 teaspoon vanilla extract

Combine sour cream, sugar, and vanilla with a rubber spatula and spread on baked batter. When oven temperature reaches 500 degrees F., bake for 10 minutes. Allow to cool and then refrigerate.

Nonbaked Ginger Cheesecake

CRUST

2 cups finely ground gingersnap crumbs

¼ cup sugar

¼ pound (1 stick) butter

Combine crust ingredients in a food processor and blend thoroughly. Line the bottom and halfway up the sides of a 9″ springform pan.

BATTER

½ pound (1 8-ounce package) cream cheese, at room temperature

1 (14-ounce) can sweetened condensed milk

⅓ cup fresh lime juice

⅓ cup ginger marmalade

1 cup sliced fresh fruit (peaches, pineapple, or nectarines are preferable)

In a mixer, beat the cream cheese until it is light and fluffy. Beat in the condensed milk and then the lime juice. Add the marmalade and stir until well blended. Line the crust with the sliced fruit. Pour the cheese mixture over the fruit and refrigerate for 2 hours, or until the cheesecake mixture is set.

Cottage Cheesecake

Preheat oven to 350 degrees F. Butter a 10-inch springform pan.

CRUST

1½   cups finely ground shortbread crumbs

½   cup sweet butter, melted

¼   cup finely chopped walnuts

Combine crumbs, butter, and walnuts in a food processor and blend thoroughly. Press firmly over the bottom of the springform pan.

BATTER

1   12-ounce container cottage cheese

1   tablespoon lemon juice

¼   teaspoon grated lemon zest

1   egg, beaten

½   cup sifted confectioners' sugar

⅛   teaspoon vanilla extract

1   teaspoon almond extract

1   cup sour cream

¼   cup grated chocolate (optional)

Drain the cottage cheese well and place in a food processor. Blend until free of large lumps. In a mixer, combine cottage cheese, lemon juice and zest, egg, sugar, and extracts. Blend thoroughly. Fold in the sour cream with the wire whisk of the mixer on the lowest speed. Pour the batter evenly into the crust and smooth the top. Bake in the preheated oven for 50 minutes. Cool well then refrigerate overnight Before serving, sprinkle the top with grated chocolate, if desired. Cake will be thin and flat.

Cheesecake for Twelve

Preheat oven to 325 degrees F. Grease a 10-inch springform pan and dust with ¼ cup cinnamon crisp crumbs.

BATTER

- 1 pound fresh ricotta cheese
- 1 pound (2 8-ounce packages) cream cheese, softened
- ½ cup margarine, softened
- 1½ cups sugar
- 4 eggs, slightly beaten
- ½ cup cornstarch
- 2 tablespoons lemon juice
- 1 teaspoon vanilla extract
- 2 cups sour cream

Blend ricotta cheese in a food processor and transfer to mixer bowl. Add cream cheese and margarine and beat at high speed until creamy. At high speed, add sugar and eggs. Reduce speed to low, then add cornstarch, lemon juice, and vanilla. Blend in sour cream at low speed. Pour into prepared pan. Bake in the preheated oven for 1 hour and 10 minutes. Turn off oven. Let cake sit in oven for 2 hours longer. Remove and cool on wire rack. Refrigerate.

German Chocolate Cheesecake

Preheat oven to 350 degrees F.

CRUST

1 cup finely ground chocolate-wafer crumbs

2 tablespoons sugar

¼ cup melted butter

Combine crumbs, sugar, and butter in a food processor and blend thoroughly. Press on bottom of a 10″ springform pan and chill.

BATTER

4 ounces sweet chocolate

1½ pounds (3 8–ounce packages) cream cheese, softened

1 cup sugar

3 eggs

½ cup strong black coffee, cooled

½ cup sour cream

⅛ teaspoon salt

1 teaspoon vanilla extract

unsweetened whipped cream and chocolate curls (optional)

Melt chocolate over simmering water in a double boiler or in a microwave oven on half power and reserve.

In a mixer, beat cream cheese until light and fluffy. Gradually beat in sugar. Add eggs, one at a time, beating well after each addition. Add chocolate, coffee, sour cream, salt, and vanilla and beat until smooth. Pour into prepared pan and bake in the preheated oven for 1 hour. Cool on a cake rack, then refrigerate. Run spatula around edge of cake to loosen. Remove sides of springform pan and garnish with whipped cream and chocolate curls, if desired.

Old-Fashioned Cheesecake

Preheat oven to 350 degrees F. Butter and flour a 9 × 9 × 2-inch baking pan.

BATTER

1½ pounds farmer cheese

½ pound (1 8-ounce package) cream cheese

1 12-ounce container dry or small-curd cottage
   cheese, drained

1½ cups sugar

1 teaspoon cinnamon

4 large eggs, beaten

1 cup white raisins

DOUGH CRUST

4 cups sifted flour

2 teaspoons baking powder

1½ cups sugar

½ cup salad oil

2 eggs, well beaten

⅓ cup ice water

2 tablespoons sugar mixed with ¼ teaspoon
   cinnamon

Whip farmer and cream cheeses together in a food processor until well blended. Add sugar and cinnamon. Blend in eggs. Fold in raisins with a spoon. Reserve.

Sift flour, baking powder, and sugar into the bowl of a food processor. Blend in oil and eggs for 3 seconds. Add water gradually through the feed tube while food processor is running until the dough forms into a soft ball. Divide the dough into three pieces, one larger than the other two. Roll out the larger piece to a 12½-inch square and line bottom and sides of pan with it. Spread half the batter over the dough. Roll out second piece of dough to an 8-inch square. Put in pan over batter. Place remaining batter on top of second layer of dough. Roll out third piece of dough into an 8½-inch square and place over batter. Press edges of bottom and top layers of dough together. Trim off excess. Make 6 slits in top layer of dough. Sprinkle sugar-cinnamon mixture over top. Bake in the preheated oven for 1 hour 10 minutes, or until fork inserted in center of cake comes out clean and top is golden brown. Cool on rack.

Pineapple Cheesecake

Preheat oven to 350 degrees F.

16 single Cinnamon Crisps, crumbled
1 cup crushed pineapple, drained
1½ pounds (3 8-ounce packages) cream cheese,
    at room temperature
1 cup sugar
4 eggs
1 teaspoon vanilla extract
1 pint sour cream

Sprinkle crumbs on bottom of a 10″ springform pan, then place pineapple over crumbs. Beat the cream cheese in mixer until smooth. Add sugar gradually, beating constantly. Add the eggs, one at a time, beating well on low speed after each addition. Add the vanilla and sour cream and beat until smooth. Pour over pineapple. Bake in the preheated oven for 1 hour. Cool on a rack. Loosen cake from side of pan with a sharp knife and release. Invert before serving.

Anise Pear Cheesecake

Preheat oven to 400 degrees F.

CRUST
- 1 cup sifted flour
- 2 tablespoons sugar
- ¼ teaspoon salt
- ½ cup softened butter
- 1 egg yolk (save egg white for batter)

Combine flour, sugar, salt, butter and egg yolk in a food processor until soft dough is formed. Pat out over bottom and up sides of a 9″ springform pan. Bake for 10 minutes. Remove from oven and reset oven temperature to 350 degrees F.

PEARS
- 3 fresh Bartlett pears
- 2 cups water
- 1 tablespoon lemon juice

Peel, core, and cut pears in half lengthwise. Heat water and lemon juice in a large skillet. Place pear halves, cut side down, in the water. Cover and cook for 2 minutes. Turn pears over, cover, and cook for 1 minute more. Remove pears from liquid and reserve.

BATTER
- 6 ounces cream cheese
- ⅓ cup sugar
- 1½ teaspoons flour
- ¼ teaspoon salt
- 1 teaspoon vanilla
- 1 teaspoon lemon juice
- 2 large eggs, separated

⅛ teaspoon cream of tartar (if egg whites are not
whipped in copper bowl)

1 egg white left over from crust

½ cup sour cream

¾ teaspoon ground anise

Soften cream cheese in a food processor. Mix sugar, flour, and salt together. Add to cream cheese and process until blended. Add vanilla, lemon juice, and egg yolks and blend until smooth. Blend in sour cream. Beat egg whites with wire whisk in a mixer until soft peaks form. Fold cheese mixture and ½ teaspoon anise into egg whites with wire whisk on lowest speed of mixer until completely combined. Turn into prepared crust and arrange poached pear halves, cut side down, on top. Sprinkle with remaining ¼ teaspoon anise. Bake in preheated oven for 50 minutes. Cool on rack, then refrigerate until ready to serve.

Ricotta Cheesecake

Preheat oven to 325 degrees F.

CRUST

- 2 cups macaroon crumbs
- 4 tablespoons butter, melted
- ¼ cup sugar

Blend together crumbs, butter, and sugar in a food processor. Press crumb mix over bottom and halfway up the sides of a 10″ springform pan. Refrigerate until batter is prepared.

BATTER

- 4 eggs
- 1 cup sugar
- 1½ pounds ricotta cheese
- ¼ cup walnut pieces
- 2 ounces white chocolate, shaved
- 2 tablespoons crystallized ginger, chopped
- 1 tablespoon flour
- 1½ teaspoons dark rum

In a mixer, beat the eggs until they become lemon colored. Gradually add sugar. Mix in ricotta cheese. Combine nuts, chocolate, and ginger and dust with flour. Add to batter and blend in. Add rum and mix until well combined. Pour into crust and bake in the preheated oven for 1 hour 15 minutes. Chill.

Index